TOP 550 AIR FRYER RECIPES

The Complete Air Fryer Recipes Cookbook for Easy, Delicious and Healthy Meals
(Air Fryer Cookbook)
BY
Francis Michael

ISBN: 978-1-952504-36-5

COPYRIGHT © 2020 by Francis Michael

All rights reserved. This book is copyright protected and it's for personal use only. Without the prior written permission of the publisher, no part of this publication should be reproduced, distributed, or transmitted in any form or by any means, including photocopying, recording, or other electronic or mechanical methods.

This book is sold with the idea that the author is not needed to render accounting, officially permitted, or otherwise, qualified services. It's recommended to seek for the services of a legal or professional, a practiced individual in the profession if advice is needed.

DISCLAIMER

The information written in this publication is geared for educational and entertainment purposes only. Concerted efforts have been made towards providing accurate, up to date and reliable complete information. The information in this book is true and complete to the best of our knowledge.

Neither the publisher nor the author takes any responsibility for any possible consequences of reading or enjoying the recipes in this book. The author and publisher disclaim any liability in connection with the use of information contained in this book. Under no circumstance will any legal responsibility or blame be apportioned against the author or publisher for any reparation, damages, or monetary loss due to the information herein, either directly or indirectly.

Table of Contents

INTRODUCTION 8
Benefits of Cooking with an Air Fryer 9
How to Use an Air Fryer 11
Step by Step Approach for Effectively Cleaning of an Air Fryer 12
    Air Fryer Cleaning Cautions: 12
Air Fryer Maintenance 13
Air Fryer Frequently Asked Questions and Answers 14
Air Fryer Cooking Charts 15
BREAKFAST RECIPES 18
    Cranberry Pecan Muffins 18
    Baked Apple 18
    Homemade Strawberry Pop Tarts 20
    French Toast Soldiers 20
    Peanut Butter and Jelly Air Fried Doughnuts 22
    Blueberry Lemon Muffin 23
    Frittata 24
    Breakfast Puffed Egg Tarts 25
    Ham and Cheese Egg Puffs 26
    Heavenly French Toast 27
    Pumpkin Muffins 28
    Hash Browns 29
    Air Fryer Bacon 30
    Breakfast Pockets 31
    Easy Omelette 32
    Flourless Broccoli Cheese Quiche 33
    Homemade Cinnamon Baked French Toast 34
    Strawberry Baked Oatmeal 34
    Blueberry & Brown Sugar Oatmeal 36
    Fluffy French Toast Sticks 37

POULTRY RECIPES 38
Honey Garlic Wings 38
Garlic Parmesan Chicken Wings 39
Spatchcock Chicken 40
Chicken Nuggets 41
Mini Turkey Pies 41
KFC Chicken Strips 43
Lemon Dijon Chicken Wings 44
Whole Roasted Lemon & Rosemary Chicken 45
Shredded Chicken 46
Roasted Chicken with Sage & Onion Stuffing 47
Chinese Chicken Wings 47
Chicken Cutlets 49
Honey BBQ Chicken Wings 50
Chicken Spiedie 51
Rotisserie Chicken 52
Greek Chicken Souvlaki 52
Spicy Chicken Burgers 54
Turkey Breast with Maple Mustard Glaze 55
KFC Popcorn Chicken 56
Chicken Wrapped In Bacon 57
Tangy Barbecue Chicken 58
Chicken Parmesan 59
Buffalo Chicken Wings 60
Tasty Chicken Drumsticks with Homemade Rub 61
Chicken Tikka 61
Leftover Turkey Burgers 63
Chicken Milanese 64
MAIN MEAL RECIPES 64
Inside Out Cheeseburgers 64

Cauliflower Chickpea Tacos 66

Roasted Vegetable Pasta Salad 67

Prosciutto, Spinach & Mushroom Pizza 67

Stir Fried Zoodles and Vegetables with Tofu 68

General Tso's Cauliflower 70

Quick Roasted Tomato Sauce with Capers and Basil 71

Curry Chickpeas 72

Chicken Wing Drumettes 73

Cauliflower Pan Pizza 74

Jalapeno Poppers 74

Sticky Mushroom Rice 76

EGG RECIPES 77

Easy Cheese Omelette 77

Southern Deviled Eggs 78

Hard Boiled Eggs 79

Egg Benedict 80

Baked Eggs 80

Thai Peanut Chicken Egg Rolls 82

Scrambled Eggs 82

Egg in Hole 84

FISH & SEAFOOD RECIPES 85

Steamed Mussels 85

Roasted Salmon with Fennel Salad 86

Spicy Fish Street Tacos with Sriracha Slaw 87

Sockeye Salmon enPapillote with Potatoes, Fennel and Dill 89

Lemon-Dill Salmon Burgers 89

Parmesan Shrimp 91

Lobster Tails 91

Bang Bang Fried Shrimp 93

Coconut Shrimp with Spicy Marmalade Sauce 93

- Air Fryer Steak 94
- Homemade Salmon Patties 95
- Maryland Jumbo Lump Crab Cakes 96
- Easiest Breaded Shrimp 97
- BLT Bites 98
- Cajun French Fries 99
- Bacon Wrapped Shrimp 100

PORK & BEEF RECIPES 101
- BBQ Ribs 101
- Honey Mustard Pork Chops 102
- Beef Stir Fry with Homemade Marinade 103
- Southern Style Fried Pork Chops 104
- Beef Hotpot 105
- Crispy Breaded Pork Chops 106
- Mongolian Beef 106
- Crispy Breaded Pork Chops 108
- Roast Beef 109
- Sausage Rolls 110
- Beef Empanadas 111

SIDE DISH RECIPES 112
- Cheese and Onion Pasties 112
- Brussels' Sprouts with Bacon 112
- Pepperoni and Cheese Pizza Chips 114
- Chewy Granola Bars 115
- Messy Sloppy Joes Cheesy Fries 116
- Spam Fritters 117
- Sweet Potato Burger Buns 118

VEGAN & VEGETARIAN 119
- Sticky Pumpkin Wedges 119
- Veggie Pakoras 120

Potato Wedges 121

Curly Fries 122

Veggie Fritters 123

Vegetable Samosas 124

Avocado on Toast 125

Grilled Tomatoes 126

Vegetable Fries 127

Pumpkin French Fries 128

French Fries 129

Crinkle Cut Chips 130

Rosemary Roast Potatoes 131

Vegan Veggie Balls 132

Apple Chips 133

Rosemary Sweet Potatoes 134

Spicy Sweet Potato Wedges 135

BURGER RECIPES 136

Lamb Burgers 136

Chicken Avocado Burgers 136

Lentil Burgers 138

Juicy Lucy Cheese Burger 138

Falafel Burger 140

Veggie Burgers 141

Bunless Burgers 142

Spicy Courgette and Chickpea Burgers 142

Chicken Burgers 144

Cauliflower Veggie Burger 145

King Whopper Burger 146

Hamburgers 146

KFC Zinger Chicken Burger 148

Nandos Beanie Burger 149

- Mediterranean Paleo Burgers 149
- Double Cheese Burger 151

SNACKS & APPETIZERS 152
- Flaky Buttermilk Biscuits 152
- Balsamic Glazed Chicken 153
- Sweet Potato Fries 153
- Crinkle Cut Chips 155
- Roasted Parsnips 156
- Cheese Toastie 157
- Buttermilk Fried Chicken 157
- Flourless Chicken Cordon Bleu 159
- Airy Breaded Chicken Bread 159
- Steak & French Fries 161
- Cheese and Bacon Chips 162
- Crispy Southern Fried Chicken 163

DESSERT RECIPES 163
- Cinnamon Rolls 163
- Apple Fries with Caramel Cream Dip 165
- Sugared Dough Dippers with Chocolate Amaretto Sauce 166
- Mini Cherry and Cheese Streusel Tartlets 166
- Brownie and Blondie Layer Bars 168
- Stuffed Apple Pies 169
- Peach and Blueberry Cobbler 170
- Chocolate Soufflés 171
- Fried Banana S'mores 172
- Midnight Nutella Banana Sandwich 173

INTRODUCTION

Benefits of Cooking with an Air Fryer

There are lots of benefits one gets using an air fryer to cook. Although there are other cooking methods but the benefits and comfort derived from cooking with an air fryer are overwhelming. The benefits are listed below:

1. **Universality:**

The air fryer has a universal feature which means it is capable of doing a multipurpose function you may want to do with it. Some people used microwave oven to fry but I tell you, the air fryer is comparable to microwave oven. It can fry chicken to the best of your taste. It may interest you to know that the air fryer can bake cake easily. Yes!!! It can bake cake very easily. Other food that you can cook with air fryer includes: all kinds of frozen foods, veggies, casserole, fish, meat etc.

One interesting feature of the air fryer is dividable basket. This helps you to cook different kinds of foods at the same time. Other extra features that could be found in some fryers include grill or baking pan, cooking rack, rotisserie rack etc. Air fryer has different sizes with different accessories that you can buy.

2. **Saves Space:**

This unit is usually easy to store and move when necessary. Unlike coffee maker, the size of air fryer is similar to it. The unit also has the ability to replace a cooker like toaster oven. Yes!!! It can replace undoubtedly. Those that are living in a small apartment with a small kitchen will benefit a lot from this unit because the size is handy and does not consume enough space in the kitchen.

3. **Gives Healthy Cooking:**

Despite the fact that the appliance can fry food with or without oil, it gives healthy cooking. It can be used to cook frozen fires, wings and onions. At the end of the cooking, you will still have crispy result even without using oil while frying. The unit can also be used to make breaded zucchini and gives you an overwhelming result.

4. **Very Easy to Clean:**

After cooking a big meal, the next thing you have to do is cleaning the appliance. There is no much work here and does not take enough of your time washing it after cooking. The air fryer only requires you to clean just a pan and a basket. Cooked food goes off to your plate. They do not get stuck to the grill pan because of the nonstick coated parts.

5. **More Efficient in Energy:**

The air fryer does not unnecessarily cause more heat inside your kitchen. When you are cooking using the air fryer, you will still feel the comfort of your room because will it not make your room to be too hot.

6. **Cooks Meal Faster:**

Due to their portability, the air fryer cooks meal faster within the specified time. Unlike a microwave which takes about 30 minutes to preheat, the air fryer can take about 10-13 minutes to come to temperature. Approximately, frozen fry can take up to about 13–15 minutes to be well cooked using the air fryer compared to a microwave oven which may take up to 40-45 minutes for the fries to be well cooked. This shows how faster the air fryer cooks. This unit is best for those who are in a hurry to prepare a meal.

7. **Simple to Use:**

Some people do not like cooking appliances that are so cumbersome to operate. The air fryer only needs just 4 simple steps to start cooking which includes: selecting the temperature, setting the cooking time, adding food and shaking it after sometimes while still cooking. The baskets make shaking of your food simple and fast as well.

How to Use an Air Fryer

The uniqueness of Air fryers lies in the fact that they can be used to deliver any fries with just a single drop of oil. This is possible with the following steps:

1. **Set the Cooking Temperature:**

Setting the temperature is always the first thing you need to do when using the air fryer. What you need to do is to convert a recipe with a suggested temperature for any deep frying using a local or traditional oven. Just reduce the temperature of air fryer by 25°F. This will give you the same result as that of a traditional oven.

For instance, if a given recipe requires the temperature to be heated up to 400°F in a traditional oven, cook at 375°F for air fryer. The rule is pertinent because air on circulation makes the cooking heat to be more intense compared to a local cooking method. Before you start cooking with the air fryer, do not forget to preheat your air fryer.

2. **Add the Ingredients with Little Oil:**

The air fryer requires that you put one or two tablespoons of oil before you put the ingredients. However, there are foods that contain lots of fat (like meatballs), it needs no extra cooking oil.

It is recommended that if you are cooking any food that has already been coated with flour and you want to get the food turn to golden brown, spray the air fryer basket first with a light cooking oil and putting the food into the air fryer basket in layers. In the other hand, there are foods that can be cooked without putting extra oil.

3. **Place the Food on the Air Fryer Basket:**

For you to be able to cook foods that are coated with flour, you place them in layer(s). There are some air fryer models that have two layer racks. Such racks that allows for two layers will enable you to cook two different things at the same time but will require a longer cooking time and will result in food that are not well cooked, that is why it is advisable to shake the air fryer after 3 or 4 minutes of the cooking time to ensure the food is cooked properly.

4. **Check Regularly for Doneness:**

Foods cook with the air fryer usually cooks faster than the foods cook with a traditional method. This is so because the temperature of the air fryer environment is being maintained consistently by the circulating air.

It should be noted that if you already know the recipe for a particular food and you wants to convert it to cook in the air fryer, you have to be checking the food regularly for doneness. For instance, if the cooking time for a given food is 20 minutes, you have to check the food after 15 minutes and then cook again for the remaining 5 minutes.

5. **Frozen French Fries Possible to Make:**

Yes! It's true. Frozen French fries could be successfully cooked using the air fryer. The impressive fact about this is that it does not necessarily require that you put oil into the air fryer before you can cook the fries. This is usually cooked at 350°F for 15 minutes. Do not fail to shake one or two times while cooking. You may add salt to it if needed and also top with preferred garnish.

Step by Step Approach for Effectively Cleaning of an Air Fryer

Air fryers are always clean. Cooking of food locally could sometimes be boring. Pans get dirty, coating board gets greasy, utensils get grimy, and other things around the fryer gets dirty. Air fryer cooking basket is closed inside the unit. This helps to avoid some drops of oil, grease, fat into the oil pan below. However, it is necessary to clean the air fryer all the time after use. In order to clean the unit, follow these simple steps:

1. If the air fryer was plugged to the wall socket, unplug it and allow it cool down.
2. Clean the outside with a wet cloth.
3. All the air fryer's components that are removable are dishwasher safe. You just need to put them into a dishwasher if you want to wash them using dishwasher. For other components put a dishwashing soap into warm water, wash the cooking tray, pan, and basket.
4. Use hot water to clean the inside of the air fryer with hot water and a cloth.
5. Check the air fryer's food basket if there is any food stuck above the heating element. Clean it.
6. After washing the cooking basket, tray and pan, ensure to allow them dry before fixing them back to the unit.

Air Fryer Cleaning Cautions:

1. Before cleaning your air fryer, ensure you wait for the last batch of food to be fully cooked if you were cooking in batches.
2. If you realize the residual foods are difficult to remove, put dishwashing soap and soak in hot water. After sometimes, wash them.
3. If there is any stuck food above the food basket, do not use utensils to remove them. The reason is that the components of your air fryer have been lined with a non-stick coating that can be scratched easily. Ensure you use a non-abrasive sponge to remove any stuck food on the cooking pan or basket.

Air Fryer Maintenance

Air fryer needs proper maintenance to extend its durability and prevent it from damaging. The maintenance steps include the following:

1. Before you start cooking make sure the air fryer is placed on a level surface. Place it in upright position.
2. Before you start cooking make sure the air fryer is clean and free from any dirt. Check inside of the unit for debris if it has been a long time you used the unit. Check the pan and basket and clean them if you found some dust.
3. Before any use, check the basket and pan for any damage. Replace any damaged parts by contacting the manufacturer.
4. Check the cables before you start using the unit. Replace any damaged cable in order to avoid unexpected injuries. This can lead to death so ensure the cables are in good condition all the time.
5. Air fryers need at least 4 inches of space behind them and 4 inches of space above them to properly vent steam and hot air while cooking and be free from unnecessary overheating. Avoid keeping the unit at close range with another appliance. Do not keep it close to the wall.

Air Fryer Frequently Asked Questions and Answers

These are the six most commonly asked questions for every beginner.

1. **What kind of food can I cook in the Air fryer?**

This is the first question that thrills the minds of beginners. Indeed there is no food you cannot cook with the air fryer. You can cook any kinds of fries, snacks, chicken, meat, and also bake cake with the air fryer. Vegetables which have to be cooked (such as carrot and broccoli) are less suitable to prepare in an Air fryer. Other vegetables can be cooked with the air fryer. A lot of people are now using the air fryer to cook frozen foods

Moreover, anything you can cook with your oven is possible to cook with your air fryer faster than the oven. If there is no preparation and cooking time available on the food packaging for air fryer, you don't have to panic. Just subtract 25ºF from the one of the oven. For instance if the oven cooking temperature is 200ºF for 20 minutes, cook in the air fryer at 175º F for 12 minutes.

2. **Where can I purchase the best Air fryer?**

Any new air fryer you purchase is the best product. Some people like to purchase a second hand product. There is no problem with that but you need to be careful so that you don't buy fake product.

3. **How much food can I cook per batch in an Air fryer?**

Air fryer has different types of models and the amount of food to be cooked per batch depends on the model of the air fryer. All the cooking baskets have their recommended amount of food you can put at a time. Do not overload the basket. If you are to put big large amount of food, it depends on the food as explained below:

Snacks: Avoid putting snacks that is more than 500 gram (18 oz.) into the cooking pan or basket at the same time. You only need to cover the bottom of the cooking basket to achieve a good result. Do not fail to shake the basket half way during cooking time so that the snacks will be properly cooked.

Rising products: This kind of food is somehow difficult to determine quantity per batch due to its rising ability. When it starts rising do not allow it to reach the level of the heat element. If that happens, it has negative impact on your air fryer.

Potatoes or any fries: You can fill the basket up to the brim level. Do not forget that large quantities could result in uneven doneness of the fries. For an improved result, you need to shake the cooking pan or basket about 2-3 times before the cooking time is completed.

Stuffed vegetables and delicate foods: These are food that you need to take them out after cooking. You have to keep enough space to enable you take them out again after cooking. Generally, to determine the amount of food to be loaded at a given batch sometimes should depend on your own judgment and base on your experience.

4. **Is it mandatory to preheat my Air Fryer?**

It depends on the type of food you are preparing. Some foods require preheating the air fryer while some foods do not require preheating the air fryer. If no preheating is done, you might have to leave your meal in slightly longer. Some foods are required to be placed in the Air fryer before it is pre-heated. For instance cooking an egg need the air fryer to be preheated. Usually, preheating the air fryer does not need much time, just 2-3 minutes.

Some air fryers beep when the air fryer come up to temperature. When the air fryer is preheated, fill the basket and set the timer to the required cooking time.

5. **Does food cooked in an Air fryer taste sweet?**

The best answer to this question is for you to try it yourself. A trial will convince you. Air fryer has the capacity to make your food look crispy on the outside and makes the inside soft. Indeed food cooked with an air fryer has a delicious taste. Air fryer is good for cooking snacks, French fries, chicken etc. Applying a little oil on the food (like chicken) will enhance the effect of your air fryer. Air fryer does not necessarily require oil to cook your food but will still give you a delicious taste.

6. **What are the important accessories the Air fryer needs?**

Most air fryers are delivered to the standard that can enable you to cook all kinds of foods. With this, you do not need extra accessories. If you still insist on getting extra accessories, you could consider buying a grill pan designed for the Air fryer. This ensures that the product is ready even faster and makes grilling meat, fish and vegetables even easier. There are other accessories which are often used with the Air fryer. They include the following:

Grill Mat: This is used to keep the basket clean. A grill mat is however easier to clean than the Air fryer basket. The grill mat can also be used in the same way as the flame distributor in order to prevent some light food items come against the heating element.

Flame Distributor: Air fryer flame distributor could be handy. The flame divider is usually used to cover the food. The heating element which is located above the basket will not have any splashes. The flame distributor also helps to prevent pine nuts, crumbs and other light food items blowing up against the heating element. A commonly used flame distributor for Air fryer XL is the Handy flame distributor of Blokker.

Bakes: There are some dishes that require being prepared in a casserole. Place the casserole out of the bottom of the pan, but in the basket. This will maintain the air circulation in the air fryer.

Air Fryer Cooking Charts

Chicken:

Chicken	Temperature (°F)	Time (Min)
Wings (2 lbs.)	400° F	12
Whole Chicken (6.5 lbs.)	360° F	75
Breast, bone in (1.25 lbs.)	370° F	25
Breasts, boneless (4 oz.)	380° F	12
Drumsticks (2.5 lbs.)	370° F	20
Thighs, bone in (2 lbs.)	380° F	22
Thighs, boneless (1.5 lbs.)	380° F	18 - 20
Legs, bone in (1.75 lbs.)	380° F	30
Tenders	360° F	8 - 10

Beef:

Beef	Temperature	Time

	(º F)	(Min)
Meatballs (1-inch)	380º F	7
Meatballs (3-inch)	380º F	10
Burger (4 oz.)	370º F	16 - 20
Fillet Mignon (8 oz.)	400º F	18
Flank Steak (1.5 lbs.)	400º F	12
London Broil (2 lbs.)	400º F	20 - 28
Beef Eye Round Roast (4 lbs.)	390º F	45 - 55
Sirloin Steaks (1-inch, 12 oz.)	400º F	9 - 14
Ribeye, bone in (1-inch, 8 oz.)	400º F	10 - 15

Fish & Seafoods:

Fish & Seafoods	Temperature (º F)	Time (Min)
Shrimp	400º F	5
Tune Steaks	400º F	7 - 10
Scallops	400º F	5 - 7
Fish Fillet (1-inch, 8 oz.)	400º F	10
Swordfish Steak	400º F	10
Calamari (8 oz.)	400º F	4
Salmon, Fillet (6 oz.)	380º F	12

Pork & Lamb

Pork & Lamb	Temperature (º F)	Time (Min)
Sausages	380º F	15
Rack of Lamb (1.5 – 2 lbs.)	380º F	22
Loin (2 lbs.)	360º F	55
Bacon (thick cut)	400º F	6 - 10
Lamb Loin Chops (1-inch thick)	400º F	8 - 10
Pork Chops, bone in (1-inch, 6.5 oz.)	400º F	12
Tenderloin (1 lb.)	370º F	15
Bacon (regular)	400º F	5 - 7

Frozen Foods

Frozen Foods	Temperature (º F)	Time (Min)
Fish Sticks (10 oz.)	400º F	10
Breaded Shrimp	400º F	9

Onion Rings (12 oz.)	400° F	8
Chicken Nuggets (12 oz.)	400° F	10
Pot Stickers (10 oz.)	400° F	8
Fish Fillets (1-inch, 10 oz.)	400° F	14
Mozzarella Sticks (11 oz.)	400° F	8
Thick French Fries (17 oz.)	400° F	18
Thin French Fries (20 oz.)	400° F	14

Vegetables

Vegetables	Temperature (°F)	Time (Min)
Onions (pearl)	400° F	10
Mushrooms (sliced ¼-inch)	400° F	5
Zucchini (1/2-inch sticks)	400° F	12
Tomatoes (halved)	350° F	10
Kale Leaves	250° F	12
Tomatoes (cherry)	400° F	4
Green Beans	400° F	5
Fennel (quartered)	370° F	15
Sweet Potato (baked)	380° F	30 - 35
Eggplant (1/2-inch cubes)	400° F	15
Corn on the cob	390° F	6
Squash (1/2-inch chunks)	400° F	12
Potatoes (baked whole)	400° F	40
Cauliflower (florets)	400° F	12
Potatoes (1-inch chunks)	400° F	12
Potatoes (small baby, 1.5 lbs.)	400° F	15
Carrots (sliced ½-inch)	380° F	15
Peppers (1-inch chunks)	400° F	15
Brussels Sprouts (halved)	380° F	15
Parsnips (1/2- inch chunks)	380° F	15
Broccoli (florets)	400° F	6
Beets (whole)	400° F	40
Asparagus (sliced 1-inch)	400° F	5

BREAKFAST RECIPES

Cranberry Pecan Muffins

Preparation Time: 10 minutes
Cooking Time: 15 minutes
Total Time: 25 minutes
Yield: 6-80 muffins
Ingredients:
- 1 ½ Cups of Almond Flour
- 2 Large eggs
- ½ Cup of fresh cranberries
- ¼ Cup of chopped pecans
- ½ Tsp. vanilla extract
- ¼ Cup of Monk fruit
- 1 Tsp. baking powder
- ¼ Cup of cashew milk
- ¼ Tsp. cinnamon
- 1/8 Tsp. salt

Cooking Instructions:
1. Put the milk, eggs and vanilla extract into the blender and blend for about 30 seconds.
2. Put almond flour, sugar, baking powder, cinnamon and salt into the blender and blend for another 45 seconds.
3. Get the blender jar out from the base and stir in ½ of the fresh cranberries and the pecans.
4. Put the mixture to silicone muffin cups. Put in each of the muffins the remains of fresh cranberries.
5. Put the muffins into the Air Fryer basket and Air-fry at 325º C for 15 minutes.
6. Remove from Air Fryer and allow it to cool on a wire rack.
7. Serve and enjoy!!!

Baked Apple

Preparation Time: 15 minutes
Cooking Time: 20 minutes
Total Time: 35 minutes
Servings: 2
Calories per Serving: 129
Ingredients:
- ¼ Tsp. cinnamon

- ¼ Tsp. nutmeg
- 1 Medium apple or pear
- 2 Tbsp. chopped walnuts
- ¼ Cup of water
- 2 Tbsp. raisins
- 1 ½ Tsp. light margarine, melted

Cooking Instructions:
1. Preheat the Air Fryer to 350° F.
2. Cut the apple or pear into half and get out some flesh around the middle.
3. Put the apple or pear in the Air Fryer.
4. Mix together margarine, cinnamon, nutmeg, walnuts and raisins in a small bowl.
5. Put the mixture into the centers of the apple or pear halves and pour some small amount of water into the pan.
6. Air-fry at 350° F for 20 minutes.
7. Serve and enjoy!!!

Homemade Strawberry Pop Tarts

Preparation Time: 10 minutes
Cooking Time: 20 minutes
Total Time: 30 minutes
Servings: 5
Calories 260 kcal

Ingredients:
- 1 Tsp. cornstarch
- 2 Refrigerated pie crusts
- 1 Oz reduced-fat Philadelphia cream cheese
- 1 Tsp. sugar sprinkles
- 1 Tsp. stevia
- ½ Cup of plain, non-fat vanilla Greek yogurt
- Olive oil or coconut oil spray
- ⅓ Cup of low-sugar strawberry preserves

Cooking Instructions:
1. Place the pie crusts on a bamboo cutting board or a flat surface.
2. Cut the 2 pie crusts into 6 rectangles (3 from each pie crust). It should be fairly long to enable you fold it to close the pop tart.
3. Mix the cornstarch and preserves in a bowl. Put a tbsp. of the preserves to the upper region of the crust.
4. Fold and close the pop tarts. Use fork to create vertical and horizontal lines along the edges. Spray olive oil in the Air Fryer and put the pop tarts.
5. Cook at 375º C for 10 minutes. After 7 minutes, flip the tarts over and cook for 3 minutes so that they are well cooked.
6. Mix the stevia, cream cheese, Greek yogurt and in a bowl to create the frosting.
7. Remove the Pop Tarts from the Air Fryer and allow them to cool. Top with some sugar and frosting.
8. Serve and enjoy!!!

French Toast Soldiers

Preparation Time: 7 minutes
Cooking Time: 10 minutes
Total Time: 17 minutes
Servings: 2

Ingredients:
- 2 Large Eggs
- ¼ Cup of Whole Milk
- 5 Slices Whole meal Bread
- Pinch Of Icing Sugar

- ¼ Cup of Brown Sugar
- 1 Tsp. Cinnamon
- Pinch Of Nutmeg
- 1 Tbsp. Honey

Cooking Instructions:
1. Divide each of your slices of bread into 4.
2. In a mixing bowl, mix all your ingredients exception of icing sugar.
3. Put each of the divided bread into the mixture to be coated and then put it into the Air Fryer.
4. Cook at 160º C for 10 minutes. Flip them over so that both sides will be well cooked. Top with some fresh berries.
5. Serve and enjoy!!!

Peanut Butter and Jelly Air Fried Doughnuts

Preparation Time: 13 minutes
Cooking Time: 10 minutes
Total Time: 23 minutes
Servings: 3

Ingredients:
Doughnuts:
- 1 Egg
- ½ Cup of buttermilk
- 1 ¼ Cups of all-purpose flour
- 1 Tsp. vanilla
- ⅓ Cup of sugar
- ½ Tsp. baking powder
- 1 Tbsp. melted butter for brushing the tops
- ½ Tsp. baking soda
- ¾ Tsp. salt
- 2 Tbsp. unsalted butter, melted and cooled

Filling:
- ½ Cup of Blueberry or strawberry jelly

Glaze:
- 2 Tbsp. milk
- 2 Tbsp. peanut butter
- ½ Cup of powdered sugar
- Pinch of sea salt

Cooking Instructions:
1. Cook jelly doughnuts and sprinkle with peanut butter glaze.
2. Whisk together the baking powder, sugar, flour, baking soda and salt in a large bowl.
3. Beat together the egg, melted butter, buttermilk and vanilla in another bowl.
4. Dig a hole by the center of the dry ingredients and pour in the wet ingredients. Mix properly with fork and stir finally with spoon.
5. Remove the dough and place on a floured surface. At first, the thickness will be much. Work the dough to come together and slice it to a 3/4" thickness.
6. Cut the dough in rounds and brush with melted butter. Cut 2" pieces of foil paper and put dough on each of the paper. Put them into the Air Fryer in batches depending on the size of your Air Fryer.
7. Cook at 350° C for 11 minutes. Whisk together and sprinkle the glaze ingredients over each doughnut.
8. Serve and enjoy!!!

Blueberry Lemon Muffin

Preparation Time: 8 minutes
Cooking Time: 12 minutes
Total Time: 20 minutes
Servings: 1 Dz.

Ingredients:
- ½ Cup of Monk Fruit
- ½ Cup of cream
- Juice from 1 lemon
- 1 Tsp. vanilla
- ¼ Cup of avocado oil
- 2 ½ Cups of self-rising flour
- 2 Eggs
- Zest from 1 lemon
- Brown sugar for topping
- 1 Cup of blueberries

Cooking Instructions:
1. Mix together the self-rising flour and sugar in small bowl. Set aside.
2. Mix cream, oil, lemon juice, eggs and vanilla in a medium bowl. Put the flour mixture to the liquid mixture and stir properly.
3. Put the batter into silicone cupcake holders. On each of the muffins, sprinkle ½ tsp. brown sugar on top.
4. Bake at 320ºC for 10 minutes, check muffins occasionally to ensure they are not cooking too fast.
5. Put a toothpick into the center of the muffin and when the toothpick comes out clean and the muffins have browned, they are done. Remove and cool.
6. Serve and enjoy!!!

Frittata

Preparation Time: 8 minutes
Cooking Time: 15 minutes
Total Time: 23 minutes
Servings: 3
Calories per Serving: 70

Ingredients:
- 1 Cup of egg whites
- 2 Tbsp. skim milk
- ¼ Cup of sliced tomato
- ¼ Cup of sliced mushrooms
- 2 Tbsp. chopped fresh chives
- Black pepper, to taste

Cooking Instructions:
1. Preheat Air Fryer at 320° F.
2. Mix all the ingredients in a bowl.
3. Transfer to a greased pan or the bottom of the Air Fryer.
4. Bake for 15 minutes or until frittata is well cooked.
5. Serve and enjoy!!!

Breakfast Puffed Egg Tarts

Preparation Time: 10 minutes
Cooking Time: 12 minutes
Total Time: 22 minutes
Servings: 4 Tarts

Ingredients:
- All-purpose flour
- 1 Sheet frozen puff pastry half a 17.3-oz/490 g package, thawed
- 3/4 Cup of shredded cheese such as Gruyère, Cheddar or Monterey Jack, divided
- 4 Large eggs
- 1 Tbsp. minced fresh parsley or chives optional

Cooking Instructions:
1. Preheat Air Fryer to 390°F (200°C).
2. On a lightly floured surface, unfold pastry sheet. Cut into 4 squares.
3. Put 2 squares in Air Fryer basket, spacing them apart. Air-fry for 10 minutes or until pastry is light golden brown.
4. Open the basket, use a metal spoon and press down the centers of each square to make an indentation.
5. Sprinkle 3 tbsp. (45 mL) cheese into each indentation and gently crack an egg into the center of each pastry.
6. Air-fry for about 12 minutes or until eggs are cooked to desired doneness. Transfer to a wire rack set over waxed paper and let cool for 5 minutes. Sprinkle with half the parsley, if desired. Serve warm.
7. Repeat steps 2 to 5 with the remaining pastry squares, cheese, eggs and parsley.
8. Serve and enjoy!!!

Ham and Cheese Egg Puffs

Preparation Time: 10 minutes
Cooking Time: 4 minutes
Total Time: 14 minutes
Servings: 5

Ingredients:
- Nonstick cooking spray
- 6 large eggs
- ¼ Tsp. 1 mL freshly ground black pepper
- ½ Cup of 125 ml grated Parmesan cheese
- ⅓ Cup of 75 ml finely chopped cooked ham
- ¼ Cup of 60 ml chopped fresh chives

Cooking Instructions:
1. Preheat oven to 450°F (230°C).
2. Separate the eggs, placing the whites in a large bowl and the yolks in 6 separate small bowls.
3. Beat egg whites and pepper using an electric mixer on high speed until stiff peaks are formed. Using a rubber spatula, fold in cheese ham and chives.
4. Spoon egg white mixture into 6 equal mounds on prepared pan, spacing them 3 inches (7.5 cm) apart. Using the back of the spoon, make a deep cavity in the center of each.
5. Bake in Air Fryer for 4 minutes. Remove pan from Air Fryer and carefully add 1 yolk to the center of each mound. Bake for 4 minutes or until yolks are just set.
6. Serve and enjoy!!!

Heavenly French Toast

Preparation Time: 8 minutes
Cooking Time: 6 minutes
Total Time: 14 minutes
Servings: 4

Ingredients:
- 6 Slices of bread
- 3 Eggs
- 2/3 Cup of milk
- 1 Tsp. of vanilla
- 1 Tbsp. of cinnamon

Cooking Instructions:
1. In a small bowl mix together the eggs, milk, cinnamon, and vanilla.
2. Then beat until the eggs are broken up and everything is mixed well.
3. Dip each piece of bread into the mixture and then shake to get the excess off and put them into your prepared pan one after the other.
4. Air Fryer for 3 minutes at 320° F. Then flip them over and Air Fry for another 3 minutes. Top with maple syrup.
5. Serve and enjoy!!!

Pumpkin Muffins

Preparation Time: 5 minutes
Cooking Time: 15 minutes
Total Time: 20 minutes
Servings: 13

Ingredients:
- 1 Cup of Pumpkin Puree
- 2 Cups of Gluten Free Oats
- ½ Cup of Honey
- 2 Medium Eggs beaten
- 1 Tsp. Coconut Butter
- 1 Tbsp. Cocoa Nibs
- 1 Tbsp. Vanilla Essence
- 1 Tsp. Nutmeg

Cooking Instructions:
1. Put all your ingredients in the blender and blend until smooth.
2. Put the muffin mix into little muffin cases, spreading it out over 12 separate ones.
3. Put in the Air Fryer and cook for 15 minutes on 180ºc.
4. Serve when cool and enjoy!!!

Hash Browns

Preparation Time: 13 minutes
Cooking Time: 15 minutes
Total Time: 28 minutes
Servings: 7 pieces

Ingredients:
- 4 Large potatoes, peeled and finely grated
- 2 Tbsp. of Corn flour
- Salt to taste
- Pepper powder to taste
- 2 Tbsp. of chili flakes
- 1 Tbsp. of garlic powder, (optional)
- 1 Tbsp. of onion Powder, (optional)
- 1 + 1 Tbsp. of vegetable oil

Cooking Instructions:
1. Soak the shredded potatoes in cold water. Drain the water. Repeat the step to drain excess starch from potatoes.
2. In a non-stick pan heat 1 tsp. vegetable oil and Air-fry shredded potatoes till cooked slightly or for 3-4 minutes.
3. Cool it down and transfer the potatoes to a plate. Put corn flour, salt, pepper, garlic, onion powder, chili flakes, and mix together roughly.
4. Spread over the plate and pat it firmly with your fingers. Refrigerate it for 20 minutes. Preheat air fryer at 180º C.
5. Remove the refrigerated potato and divide into equal pieces with a knife.
6. Brush the wire basket of the Air Fryer with little oil and put the hash brown pieces in the basket and fry for 15 minutes at 180º C.
7. Remove the basket and flip the hash browns at 6 minutes so that they are air fried uniformly. Top with ketchup.
8. Serve hot and enjoy!!!

Air Fryer Bacon

Preparation Time: 8 minutes
Cooking Time: 3 minutes
Total Time: 11 minutes
Servings: 4

Ingredients:
- 6 strips of bacon

Cooking Instructions:
1. Place the bacon in the bottom of your Air Fryer.
2. Put the wire rack over your bacon that came with Air Fryer.
3. Cook at 390º C for 3 minutes. Open up the Air Fryer and flip the bacon.
4. Put the Air Fryer basket back and cook for another 3 minutes or until however crispy you like your bacon.
5. Serve and enjoy!!!

Breakfast Pockets

Preparation Time: 5 minutes
Cooking Time: 3 minutes
Total Time: 8 minutes
Servings: 3

Ingredients:
- One box puff pastry sheets
- 5 Eggs
- ½ Cup of sausage crumbles, cooked
- ½ Cup of bacon, cooked
- ½ Cup of cheddar cheese, shredded

Cooking Instructions:
1. Cook eggs as regular scrambled eggs. Add meat to the egg mixture while you cook (if desired).
2. Spread out puff pastry sheets on a cutting board and cut out rectangles with a cookie cutter or knife making sure they are all uniform so they will fit nicely together.
3. Spoon preferred egg, meat, and cheese combos onto half of the pastry rectangles. Place a pastry rectangle on top of the mixture and press edges together with a fork to seal.
4. Spray with spray oil if you want a shiny, smooth pastry although it is optional.
5. Place breakfast pockets in the Air Fryer basket and cook for 8-10 minutes at 370° C. You have to be checking it occasionally or every 3 minutes.
6. Serve and enjoy!!!

Easy Omelette

Preparation Time: 10 minutes
Cooking Time: 10 minutes
Total Time: 20 minutes
Servings: 3

Cooking Ingredients:
- 2 Eggs
- ¼ Cup of milk
- Pinch of salt
- Fresh meat and veggies, diced (You may use red bell pepper, green onions, ham and mushrooms)
- 1 Tsp. McCormick Good Morning Breakfast Seasoning – Garden Herb
- ¼ Cup of shredded cheese (I used cheddar and mozzarella)

Cooking Instructions:
1. In a small bowl, mix the eggs and milk until well combined.
2. Put a pinch of salt and veggies to the egg mixture.
3. Pour the egg mixture into a well-greased 6"x3" pan. Put the pan into the basket of the Air Fryer.
4. Cook at 350° F for 8-10 minutes. While it's still cooking, sprinkle the breakfast seasoning onto the eggs and sprinkle the cheese over the top.
5. Use a thin spatula to loosen the omelet from the sides of the pan and transfer to a plate. Garnish with extra green onions (optional).
6. Serve and enjoy!!!

Flourless Broccoli Cheese Quiche

Preparation Time: 10 minutes
Cooking Time: 40 minutes
Total Time: 50 minutes
Servings: 2

Ingredients:
- 1 Large Broccoli
- 3 Large Carrots
- 1 Large Tomato
- 100g Cheddar Cheese grated
- 20g Feta Cheese
- 150 ml Whole Milk
- 2 Large Eggs
- 1 Tsp. Parsley
- 1 Tsp. Thyme
- Salt & Pepper

Cooking Instructions:
1. Chop up your broccoli into florets. Peel and dice your carrots.
2. Place your carrots and broccoli in Air Fryer and cook for 20 minutes or until soft.
3. In a measuring jug add all your seasonings. Crack the eggs into the jug and mix well.
4. Add the milk a bit at a time until you have a pale mixture. When the steamer has finished, drain the vegetables.
5. Line the bottom of your quiche dish with them. Layer with the tomatoes and then add your cheese on top.
6. Pour the liquid over and then put more cheese on top.
7. Place it in the Air Fryer and cook for 20 minutes at 180º C.
8. Serve immediately!!!

Homemade Cinnamon Baked French Toast

Preparation Time: 10 minutes
Cooking Time: 15 minutes
Total Time: 25 minutes
Servings: 5

Ingredients:

- 2 Cans Pillsbury Cinnamon Rolls
- ¼ Cup of melted butter
- 2 Eggs
- ½ Cup of cream
- 3 Tsp. cinnamon
- 1 Tsp. nutmeg
- 1 Tsp. vanilla extract

Cooking Instructions:

1. Melt the butter, and then use it to spread on the Air Fryer safe pan.
2. Cup the cinnamon rolls into 4ths, then spread them on the Air Fryer pan.
3. In a small bowl, mix the eggs, cream, cinnamon, nutmeg and vanilla extract. Pour the mixture over the cinnamon rolls.
4. Place your Air Fryer safe pan into the air fryer basket and set the time for 12 minutes at 350º F. After 12 minutes check your casserole.
5. Make sure it's well cooked but if it does not cooked well add another 3 minutes, and check every 3 minutes until it's completely cooked.
6. Remove from Air Fryer basket, and immediately pour the icing (that comes with the rolls).
7. Serve and enjoy!!!!

Strawberry Baked Oatmeal

Preparation Time: 15 minutes
Cooking Time: 12 minutes
Total Time: 27 minutes
Servings: 4

Ingredients:

- 1 Cup of milk
- 1 Egg
- 2 Cup of mixed berries, divided
- 1 Cup of rolled oats
- ½ Tsp. of baking powder

- ½ Tsp. of ground cinnamon
- ⅓ Tsp. of salt
- ⅙ Cup of brown sugar
- ⅛ Cup of slivered almonds

Cooking Instructions:
1. In a small bowl, mix together the egg and milk.
2. In another bowl, mix the oatmeal, brown sugar, salt, baking powder, cinnamon. Spray your Air Fryer safe pan with non-stick cooking spray.
3. Put ¼ cup of fruit on the bottom, pour the oatmeal mixtures in, and then pour the egg/milk mixture over that. Allow it to cool for about 10 minutes. Then add more fruit on top of that.
4. Sprinkle almonds and nutmeg on top. Set the pan in your Air Fryer and cook for 10 minutes at 320º F. Check after 10 minutes to see how it's doing.
5. When it's done, remove from the Air Fryer and let it cool for few minutes.
6. Serve and enjoy!!!

Blueberry & Brown Sugar Oatmeal

Preparation Time: 10 minutes
Cooking Time: 10 minutes
Total Time: 20 minutes
Servings: 2

Ingredients:
- 1 Cup of milk
- 1 Egg
- 1 Cup rolled oats
- ½ Tsp. baking powder
- ½ Tsp. cinnamon
- ½ Tsp. nutmeg
- ¾ Cup of brown sugar

Cooking Instructions:
1. In a small bowl, mix together the egg and milk.
2. Spray your Air Fryer safe pan with non-stick cooking spray.
3. In another bowl mix together the rolled oats, baking powder, cinnamon, nutmeg and brown sugar.
4. Place about ¼ cup of blueberries on the bottom. Pour the egg and milk mixture over it.
5. Pour the oat mixture on top of it. Allow to cool for about 10 minutes. Top with the rest of the blueberries.
6. Place in your Air Fryer at a temperature of 320º F for 10 minutes. After 10 minutes check your dish if it is done.
7. Serve and enjoy!!!

Fluffy French Toast Sticks

Preparation Time: 7 minutes
Cooking Time: 5 minutes
Total Time: 12 minutes
Servings: 3

Ingredients:
- 4 Slices of bread
- 2 Eggs
- ¼ Cup of milk
- ¼ Cup of brown sugar
- 1 Tsp. of vanilla
- 1 Tbsp. of honey
- 1 Tbsp. of cinnamon
- ½ Tsp. of nutmeg

Cooking Instructions:
1. Slice each bread slice into 4 pieces.
2. In a small bowl mix together the eggs, milk, brown sugar, honey, vanilla, cinnamon, and nutmeg, beat until the eggs are broken up and everything is mixed well.
3. Dip each French toast stick into the mixture and then shake to get the excess off. As you are doing this, line them up in your Air Fryer Basket.
4. Place in your Air Fryer at a temperature of 320° F for 2 minutes. Flip them over and do another 3 minutes.
5. Top with maple syrup.
6. Serve and enjoy!!!

POULTRY RECIPES

Honey Garlic Wings

Preparation Time: 10 minutes
Cooking Time: 24 minutes
Total Time: 34 minutes
Servings: 5

Ingredients:
- ½ pound of chicken wings
- ½ cup of soy sauce
- ½ cup of brown sugar
- 2 teaspoons of minced garlic
- 2 teaspoons of ground ginger
- ½ cup of honey
- 3 Tbsp. cornstarch (use as a thicker)

Cooking Instructions:
1. Place the chicken wings in the Air Fryer and cook for 12 minutes at 400° F.
2. Flip them and cook for another 12 minutes.
3. Prepare the sauce in a saucepan, add your soy sauce, garlic, ginger, brown sugar, honey and stir.
4. If you want your sauce to be heavier, stir in the cornstarch, Mix well and remove from heat.
5. Coat all sides with the sauce when the chicken wings are done.
6. Serve immediately and enjoy!!!

Garlic Parmesan Chicken Wings

Preparation Time: 15 minutes
Cooking Time: 24 minutes
Total Time: 39 minutes
Servings: 4

Ingredients:
- 2 Pounds chicken wings
- Garlic Parmesan Sauce
- ¾ Cup grated Parmesan cheese
- 2 Tbsp. minced garlic
- 1 Tbsp. parsley
- 1 Tsp. salt
- ¼ Tsp. pepper

Instructions:
1. Preheat the Air Fryer to 400°F.
2. In a small bowl, mix together the cheese, garlic, parsley, salt, pepper and then toss the wings in the coating.
3. Place about half of the chicken wings in the fry basket and insert into the Air Fryer.
4. Cook for about 14 minutes or until the skin is browned and crisp.
5. After 14 minutes, turn the other side of the chicken wings, and set it for another 14 minutes.
6. This is a good way to make sure that all sides are cooked without any burnt on either sides.
7. Repeat with all the wings, until you are done with the batch.

Spatchcock Chicken

Preparation Time: 3 minutes
Cooking Time: 50 minutes
Total Time: 53 minutes
Servings: 4
Calories: 400 kcal

Ingredients:

- 0.9 Kilo Spatchcock Chicken
- 1 Tbsp. Garlic Puree
- 2 Tsp. Olive Oil
- 1 Tsp. Mixed Herbs
- Salt & Pepper

Cooking Instructions:

1. Mix together all the seasonings, the olive oil and the garlic puree until it forms a really thick paste.
2. Place the spatchcock chicken in the Air Fryer on the Air Fryer grill pan. Using your hands, rub the garlic paste over all visible skin so that you have a good coating.
3. Cook in the Air Fryer at 180º C for 25 minutes on each side respectively.
4. Serve warm with rice and salad.

Chicken Nuggets

Preparation Time: 10 minutes
Cooking Time: 8 minutes
Total Time: 18 minutes
Servings: 5

Ingredients:
- 1 Pound of chicken, cut up into chunks
- 1 Egg
- 1 Cup of milk
- 1 Cup of flour
- 1 Cup of panko
- 2 Tsp. of onion powder
- 2 Tsp. of salt
- 1 Tsp. of pepper
- 1 Tbsp. of paprika

Cooking Instructions:
1. Remove your chicken from the refrigerator, cut all the fat off and then cut them into 1 inch chunks.
2. In a small mixing bowl, put the flour, panko, onion powder, salt, pepper and paprika. Mix it all together.
3. In another bowl beat the egg and milk together and then dip the chicken into the egg-milk mixture.
4. Add the chicken in a bowl and place in the refrigerator for about an hour. Roll the chicken into the panko mixture.
5. Put in the Air Fryer Basket. Set your Air Fryer to 370º C and set the timer to 4 minutes.
6. After the time is up, flip the chicken and cook for another 4 minutes.
7. You may spray the chicken nuggets with non-stick cooking spray, both times.
8. Serve with dipping sauce and enjoy!!!

Mini Turkey Pies

Preparation Time: 2 minutes
Cooking Time: 10 minutes
Total Time: 12 minutes
Servings: 6

Ingredients:
- 8 Slices Filo Pastry
- 50g Shredded Turkey
- 1 Small Egg beaten

- 50ml Coconut Milk
- 50ml Whole Milk
- 200ml Homemade Tomato Sauce
- 20ml Turkey Stock
- 1 Tsp. Oregano
- 1 Tbsp. Coriander
- Salt and Pepper

Cooking Instructions:
1. In a small mixing bowl, put your wet ingredients apart from the egg and mix well.
2. Add the turkey and seasoning. Mix again and set side.
3. Line your little pie cases with a little flour to avoid sticking and then line with the filo pastry.
4. Aim for one sheet of filo for each pie you are doing and keep it at the center so that you can then fold over the spare pastry for the top of the pie.
5. Add the mixture to each mini pie pot so that they are ¾ full.
6. Cover the top with the remaining pastry and then brush the egg along the top.
7. Place in the Air Fryer for 10 minutes on 180º C.
8. Serve immediately and enjoy!!!

KFC Chicken Strips

Preparation Time: 12 minutes
Cooking Time: 12 minutes
Total Time: 24 minutes
Servings: 7

Ingredients:
- 1 Chicken Breast chopped into strips
- 15ml Desiccated Coconut
- 15ml Plain Oats
- 5ml KFC Spice Blend
- 75ml Bread Crumbs
- 50g Plain Flour
- 1 Small Egg beaten
- Salt & Pepper

Cooking Instructions:
1. Chop up your chicken breast into strips.
2. In a small mixing bowl, put your coconut, oats, KFC spice blend, bread crumbs and salt and pepper.
3. In another small mixing bowl, put your egg and in another small bowl, put your plain flour.
4. Put your strips in the plain flour, then in the egg and finally in the spicy layer.
5. Place in the Air Fryer at 180º C and cook for 8 minutes and then cook for a further 4 minutes on 160º C so that the chicken has plenty of time to cook in the center.
6. Serve and enjoy!!!

Lemon Dijon Chicken Wings

Preparation Time: 10 minutes
Cooking Time: 28 minutes
Total Time: 38 minutes
Servings: 6

Ingredients:
- 2 Lb. chicken wings
- Lemon Dijon Sauce:
- 4 Tbsp. olive oil
- 1 Tbsp. lemon juice
- 2 Tbsp. Dijon mustard
- 2 Tsp. minced garlic
- 1 Tsp. salt
- 1 Tsp. pepper

Cooking Instructions:
1. Preheat the air fryer to 400° F.
2. In a small bowl, mix together the olive oil, lemon juice, Dijon mustard, garlic, salt, and pepper and then toss the wings in the coating.
3. Place about half of the chicken wings in the fry basket and insert into the Air Fryer.
4. Cook for about 14 minutes or until the skin is browned and crisp.
5. After 14 minutes, turn the other side of the chicken wings, and set it for another 14 minutes.
6. This is a good way to make sure that all sides are cooked without any burnt on either sides.
7. Repeat with all the wings, until you are done with all the batches.
8. Serve and enjoy!!!

Whole Roasted Lemon & Rosemary Chicken

Preparation Time: 10 minutes
Cooking Time: 50 minutes
Total Time: 1 hour
Servings: 5

Ingredients:
- 5 Lb. whole chicken (size will depend on your Air Fryer)
- 2 Sprigs of rosemary
- Juice of 2 lemons

Cooking Instructions:
1. Clean the chicken, then rub the lemon over the chicken.
2. Sprinkles the rosemary over it. (You may place the used lemons in the cavity of the chicken).
3. Spray your chicken with olive oil sprayer, and set the temperature to 330º F for 30 minutes.
4. After the 30 minutes is up, flip the chicken and cook for another 20 minutes.
5. Do not forget that if you eat raw meat, it is dangerous.
6. Use a meat thermometer for making sure your internal temperature of the chicken is 165º F.
7. Serve and enjoy!!!

Shredded Chicken

Preparation Time: 2 minutes
Cooking Time: 15 minutes
Total Time: 17 minutes
Servings: 2 Chicken Breasts
Calories: 583 kcal

Ingredients:
- 2 Large Chicken Breasts
- 1 Tsp. Honey
- 1 Tsp. Mustard
- 1 Tsp. Garlic Puree
- Salt and Pepper

Cooking Instructions:
1. Put all the marinade ingredients into the Air Fryer baking pan and stir until well mixed.
2. Put the chicken breasts into the marinade and season the top of the chicken breasts with salt and pepper.
3. Cook inside the Air Fryer for 15 minutes at 180º C. After 5 minutes of cooking time, slice the chicken breasts into three.
4. Pour over some of the marinade into the gaps. This will enhance the flavor and allow the chicken breasts to cook quickly.
5. When the chicken is cooked, place it onto a chopping board and allow it to cool for a minute or two.
6. Using a knife and fork to shred the chicken into small pieces.
7. Serve immediately and enjoy!!!

Roasted Chicken with Sage & Onion Stuffing

Preparation Time: 10 minutes
Cooking Time: 50 minutes
Total Time: 1 hour
Servings: 5
Calories: 753 kcal
Ingredients:
Whole Chicken:
- 2.5 Tbsp. Olive Oil
- 1 Tbsp. Parsley
- Salt and Pepper

The Stuffing:
- 450g Sausage meat
- 1 Onion
- 4 Tbsp. Breadcrumbs
- 2 Tsp. Butter
- 1 Tbsp. Sage
- 1 Tsp. Thyme
- Salt and pepper

Cooking Instructions:
1. Make your sage and onion stuffing. Peel and thinly dice the onion.
2. Mix it together in a bowl along with the rest of your sage and onion stuffing ingredients. Stuff the sage and onion stuffing into the cavity of your roasted chicken.
3. Massage the olive oil into the breast sides of the chicken until all skin has been massaged. Season the oily areas with salt, pepper and parsley.
4. Turn the roasted chicken over and place in the Air Fryer breast side down. While it is in the Air Fryer rub the bottom skin areas of the chicken breast in the olive oil, followed by the same seasonings.
5. Cook your Air Fryer roasted chicken breast side down for 25 minutes at 180º C. When the Air Fryer beeps using your tongs, turn it over.
6. Cook it for the same amount of time and at the same temperature on the other side. Serve immediately and enjoy!!!

Chinese Chicken Wings

Preparation Time: 5 minutes
Cooking Time: 25 minutes
Total Time: 30 minutes
Servings: 5
Ingredients:
- 1 Cup of soy sauce
- 1 Cup of brown sugar
- 1 Tbsp. of garlic powder

- 2 Lbs. of chicken wings

Cooking Instructions:
1. Add the soy sauce, brown sugar, and garlic powder into a small saucepan, boil it and remember to stir because it will burn quickly.
2. Pour the sauce over the chicken wings, cover and refrigerate for at least 30 minutes.
3. Preheat your Air Fryer to 360º F and cook for 15 minutes and then turn them over and then Cook for another 10 minutes.
4. Do not forget to use your thermometer and check for doneness, eating uncooked chicken is dangerous.
5. Serve immediately and enjoy!!!

Chicken Cutlets

Preparation Time: 4 minutes
Cooking Time: 10 minutes
Total Time: 14 minutes
Servings: 6
Calories: 430 kcal

Ingredients:
- 3 Medium Chicken Breasts
- 2 Medium Eggs beaten
- 200g Gluten Free Oats
- 2 Tbsp. Dried Garlic
- 1 Tbsp. Mustard Powder
- 1 Tbsp. Basil
- 25g Parmesan
- Salt and Pepper

Cooking Instructions:
1. Divide your chicken into 6 pieces.
2. Blend half of your gluten free oats until they resemble fine oats.
3. Create your production line. In a first bowl put your egg. In another bowl put your blended oats. In a third bowl put your unblended oats.
4. Put to the blended oats ¼ of the unblended oats along with salt, pepper and mustard powder.
5. Add to the unblended oats ¼ of the blended oats along with salt, pepper, dried garlic, parmesan cheese and basil.
6. Add the chicken cutlets in the fake flour, the egg and then the fake breadcrumbs.
7. Cook 2 at a time in the Air Fryer for 11 minutes at 175º C.
8. Serve immediately!!!

Honey BBQ Chicken Wings

Preparation Time: 5 minutes
Cooking Time: 24 minutes
Total Time: 29 minutes
Servings: 6

Ingredients:
- 12 Chicken wings
- 1 Tsp. of salt
- 1 Tsp. of pepper
- ½ Cup of flour
- ½ Cup of barbecue sauce
- ½ Cup of honey

Cooking Instructions:
1. Preheat the air fryer to 350° F.
2. Put your wings into a bowl, and pour the flour, salt, and pepper on them. Coat them on all sides with the flour.
3. Put your wings into the Air Fryer and cook them 12 minutes and then turn them over and cook for another 12 minutes.
4. Pour the honey and BBQ sauce into a bowl and mix together.
5. When the wings are done, place them in the BBQ Sauce and Honey mixture and coat them.
6. Serve immediately and enjoy!!!

Chicken Spiedie

Preparation Time: 10 minutes
Cooking Time: 30 minutes
Total Time: 40 minutes
Servings: 4

Ingredients:
- Homemade Bread Rolls
- 2 Chicken Breasts
- 1 Large Lemon
- 4 Garlic Cloves
- 1 Tbsp. Olive Oil
- 2 Tbsp. Oregano
- 1 Tbsp. Basil
- Fresh Mint
- Salt and Pepper

Cooking Instructions:
1. Dice your chicken into big sized chunks and place them into a mixing bowl. Squeeze the juice from the lemon into the bowl.
2. Peel and thinly slice the garlic and add it too. Put the olive oil and the seasoning. Mix well with your hands until the chicken is well coated.
3. Fill the skewers with the chicken and then place in the fridge overnight. Next is to make the bread.
4. Use our bread recipe and instead form that into cute hotdog shapes. When you have made it place the four bread rolls into the Air Fryer and cook for 15 minutes at 185ºC.
5. When they are done put them to one side and cook the chicken for 15 minutes on 185º C.
6. Fill the bread rolls with the skewed chicken and add some homemade mayonnaise to it.
7. Serve and enjoy!!!

Rotisserie Chicken

Preparation Time: 2 minutes
Cooking Time: 40 minutes
Total Time: 42 minutes
Servings: 5
Ingredients:
Whole Chicken
Brine:
- 1 Chicken OXO Cube
- 1 Tbsp. Paprika
- 2 Tsp. Thyme
- Salt and Pepper

Chicken Rub:
- 1 Tbsp. Olive Oil
- 1 Tbsp. Paprika
- 1 Tsp. Celery Salt
- Salt and Pepper

Cooking Instructions:
1. Add all of your brine ingredients into your freezer bag. Put the whole chicken and then fill with cold water until the chicken is fully covered.
2. Zip it up and refrigerate it overnight. The next day when you are ready to cook your Air Fryer Rotisserie Chicken.
3. Remove the chicken from the bag, remove the giblets, remove the brine stock and pat dry your whole chicken with some kitchen towel.
4. Make your chicken rub in a small bowl. Add your whole chicken in the Air Fryer (breast side down) and rub ½ of the olive oil and ½ of the chicken rub into all visible skin.
5. Cook the chicken for 20 minutes at 180º C. After 20 minutes turn over with kitchen tongs, put the remainder of the oil and the chicken rub onto the other side of the chicken.
6. Cook again for another 20 minutes at the same temperature. Serve immediately!!!

Greek Chicken Souvlaki

Preparation Time: 5 minutes
Cooking Time: 9 minutes
Total Time: 14 minutes
Servings: 2
Ingredients:
- 1 Chicken Breast
- 1 Small Lemon juice and rind
- 3 Garlic Cloves
- 1 Tsp. Coconut Oil

- 1 Tsp. Greek Yoghurt
- 1 Tbsp. Oregano
- Pinch Thyme
- Salt and Pepper

Cooking Instructions:
1. Chop your chicken breast into medium sized pieces. Peel and thinly dice your fresh garlic.
2. Add the garlic, seasoning and lemon into a mixing bowl with your chicken and mix well with your hands.
3. Add it into the storage container and refrigerate overnight. The next day, toss the chicken in the coconut oil and the Greek yoghurt.
4. Place the chicken onto skewers and cook for 9 minutes at 180º C in the grill pan inside the Air Fryer.
5. Turn with tongs after the half way point so that both sides can have a crispy grill like coating.
6. Serve with fresh oregano.

Spicy Chicken Burgers

Preparation Time: 5 minutes
Cooking Time: 10 minutes
Total Time: 15 minutes
Servings: 4
Calories: 342 kcal

Ingredients:
- 2 Large Chicken Breasts
- 2 Tsp. Paprika
- Salt and Pepper

Flour Coating:
- 200g Plain Flour
- ½ Tsp. Cayenne Pepper
- 1 Tbsp. Onion Powder
- 1 Tbsp. Garlic Powder
- 1 Tbsp. Paprika
- 1 Tsp. Basil

Hot Pepper Sauce:
- 1 Can Tinned Tomatoes
- 1 Tsp. Cayenne Pepper
- 1 Tsp. Garlic Powder
- 1 Tbsp. Paprika
- Handful Black Peppercorns

Cooking Instructions:
1. Put all your hot pepper sauce ingredients into a blender and blend until smooth. Place it into a large bowl.
2. In another bowl add your flour and put the spicy flour ingredients. Mix with a fork until the flour has a glow to it from the seasonings.
3. Butterfly the chicken breasts so that your 2 chicken breasts become 4 pieces. Season the top of the chicken with salt, pepper and paprika.
4. Put the chicken into the flour bowl, then into the hot pepper sauce bowl and then put it back into the flour.
5. Make sure with each coating that you make sure the chicken is drowning in it.
6. Add in the Air Fryer grill pan, attach to the Air Fryer and cook for 10 minutes at 180ºC.
7. Serve inside burger buns with salad garnish and mayonnaise.

Turkey Breast with Maple Mustard Glaze

Preparation Time: 15 minutes
Cooking Time: 54 minutes
Total Time: 1 hour 9 minutes
Servings: 6

Ingredients:

- 2 Tsp. olive oil
- 5 Lb. whole turkey breast
- 1 Tsp. dried thyme
- ½ Tsp. dried sage
- ½ Tsp. smoked paprika
- 1 Tsp. salt
- ½ Tsp. freshly ground black pepper
- ¼ Cup maple syrup
- 2 Tbsp. Dijon mustard
- 1 Tbsp. butter

Cooking Instructions:

1. Pre heat Air Fryer to 350° F. Rub the olive oil all over the turkey breast. Mix together the thyme, sage, paprika, salt and pepper.
2. Rub the outside of the turkey breast with the spice mixture. Transfer the seasoned turkey breast to the Air Fryer basket and Air-fry at 350° F for 25 minutes.
3. Turn the turkey breast on its side and Air-fry for another 12 minutes. Turn the turkey breast on the opposite side and Air-fry for another 12 minutes.
4. When fully cooked, the internal temperature of the turkey breast should reach 165°F. While the turkey is Air-Frying, mix the maple syrup, mustard and butter in a small saucepan.
5. When the cooking time is up, return the turkey breast to an upright position and rub the glaze all over the turkey.
6. Air-fry for a final 5 minutes, until the skin is nicely browned and crispy. Let the turkey rest, for at least 5 minutes before slicing.
7. Serve and enjoy!!!

KFC Popcorn Chicken

Preparation Time: 10 minutes
Cooking Time: 12 minutes
Total Time: 22 minutes
Servings: 11
Calories: 48 kcal

Ingredients:
- 1 Chicken Breast
- 2ml KFC Spice Blend
- 60ml Bread Crumbs
- 1 Small Egg beaten
- 50g Plain Flour
- Salt and Pepper

Cooking Instructions:
1. In the food processor blend your chicken until it resembles minced chicken.
2. Set up a factory line with a bowl with your flour and a second bowl with your beaten egg.
3. In a third bowl mix together your KFC spice blend, salt and pepper and bread crumbs.
4. Make your minced chicken into balls and roll in the flour, the egg and then the spiced bread crumbs. Put them in the form of factory line up.
5. Place in the Air Fryer at 180º C for about 12 minutes.
6. Serve and enjoy!!!

Chicken Wrapped In Bacon

Preparation Time: 3 minutes
Cooking Time: 15 minutes
Total Time: 18 minutes
Servings: 6
 Calories: 104 kcal

Ingredients:
- 6 Back Bacon
- 1 Chicken Breast
- 1 Tbsp. Garlic Soft Cheese

Cooking Instructions:
1. Chop up your chicken breast into six bite sized pieces.
2. Lay out your bacon rashers and spread them with a small layer of soft cheese.
3. Place your chicken on top of the cheese and roll them up. Secure them with a cocktail stick.
4. Place them in the Air Fryer and cook for 15 minutes at 180º C.
5. Serve immediately!!!

Tangy Barbecue Chicken

Preparation Time: 10 minutes
Cooking Time: 15 minutes
Total Time: 25 minutes
Servings: 4

Ingredients:
- 5 Tbsp. of balsamic vinegar
- ¼ Cup of brown sugar
- 3 Tbsp. of soy sauce
- 3 Tbsp. of olive oil
- 3 Tbsp. of Dijon mustard
- 4 Boneless Skinless Chicken Breast

Cooking Instructions:
1. Mix all of the sauce ingredients in a bowl, mix well.
2. Put your chicken, and let marinade for about 30 minutes. (Put the chicken in the refrigerator).
3. Put the chicken directly on the rack in the Air Fryer.
4. Cook for about 15 minutes at 380º F.
5. Serve immediately!!!

Chicken Parmesan

Preparation Time: 10 minutes
Cooking Time: 22 minutes
Total Time: 32 minutes
Servings: 4

Ingredients:
- 2 Eggs, cracked and mixed in a bowl
- 1 Cup of breadcrumbs or panko
- 1 Tsp. of Italian seasoning
- 5 Tbsp. of vegetable oil
- 2 Pieces of chicken breast
- 1 Cup of marinara sauce
- ½ Cup of shredded mozzarella cheese

Cooking Instructions:
1. Pre-heat your Air Fryer to 350º F.
2. In a small bowl, break your eggs and mix them. In another bowl, mix together the breadcrumbs or panko, Italian seasoning and oil.
3. Dip the chicken into the egg mixture and then into the breadcrumb mixture and then place them in your Air Fryer basket.
4. Cook for about 18 minutes at 350º F. After 10 minutes, flip your chicken and use non-stick cooking spray and spray the side.
5. When the chicken is done, remove the chicken breasts. Put your chicken in an Air Fryer safe bowl, and then poured the marinara sauce and then sprinkled the cheese over it.
6. Air Fry for another 4 minutes just to melt the cheese.
7. Serve and enjoy!!!

Buffalo Chicken Wings

Preparation Time: 10 minutes
Cooking Time: 36 minutes
Total Time: 46 minutes
Servings: 5
Ingredients:
- 16 Chicken Wings Frozen
- ½ Cup butter melted
- ½ Cup hot sauce
- Tbsp. white vinegar
- 2 Tsp. Worcestershire sauce
- 1 Tsp. granulated garlic
- ½ Cup flour

Cooking Instructions:
1. Preheat your Air Fryer to 370º F.
2. Add flour to a large mixing bowl, and then coat your chicken wings. Add your coated frozen wings to the Air Fryer Basket.
3. In a small saucepan, mix together the butter, hot sauce, white vinegar, Worcestershire sauce, and garlic.
4. Just simmer until everything is combined and the butter is melted. Cook for 12 minutes at 370º F.
5. Turn the sides over and cook for another 12 minutes. Open and turn them over again. Cook for another 12 minutes at 370º F.
6. Remove the chicken and add them to a large mixing bowl. Pour the sauce over them.
7. Serve immediately!!!

Tasty Chicken Drumsticks with Homemade Rub

Preparation Time: 5 minutes
Cooking Time: 16 minutes
Total Time: 21 minutes
Servings: 5

Ingredients:
- 1 Tsp. of salt
- 1 Tsp. of black pepper
- 2 Tbsp. House Montreal Chicken Seasoning
- 1½ Lbs. of chicken drumsticks
- Oil, to rub on the chicken, I didn't measure

Cooking Instructions:
1. Rub your oil, over the chicken. Season both sides of the chicken with the seasonings above.
2. Preheat the air fryer to 200º C for about 4 minutes.
3. Cook your chicken for 5 minutes, then flip to the other side and cook for another 5 minutes.
4. After the 10 minutes are up, reduce your heat to 150ºC and cook for another 6 minutes.
5. Let the chicken rest for a couple of minutes and then flip onto a serving plate.
6. Serve and enjoy!!!

Chicken Tikka

Preparation Time: 3 minutes
Cooking Time: 10 minutes
Total Time: 13 minutes
Servings: 4

Ingredients:
- 2 Large Chicken Breasts
- Chicken Tikka Marinade:
- 1 Tsp. Grated Ginger
- 2 Tsp. Garlic Puree
- ½ Small Diced Onion
- Pinch Of Chili
- 2 Tsp. Garam Masala

- 2 Tsp. Paprika
- 2 Tsp. Turmeric
- 2 Tsp. Cumin
- Juice and Rind of 1 Lemon
- 300ml Greek Yoghurt

Cooking Instructions:
1. In a mixing bowl add all your chicken tikka marinade ingredients. Mix them well.
2. Put the chicken breasts and allow it to marinade overnight.
3. The next day remove the chicken breasts from the marinade and put them on a chopping board. Chop into chicken tikka bite shapes.
4. Cook in the Air Fryer grill pan inside of the Air Fryer for 10 minutes at 180º C
5. Serve warm and enjoy!!!

Leftover Turkey Burgers

Preparation Time: 3 minutes
Cooking Time: 20 minutes
Total Time: 23 minutes
Servings: 12

Ingredients:
- 500g Roast Dinner Leftovers
- 100g Cheddar Cheese
- 100g Gluten Free Oats

Cooking Instructions:
1. Preheat the Air Fryer to 180º C.
2. Put your leftovers in a mixing bowl. Put the oats and cheese. Mix well until combined.
3. Put them in the Air Fryer for 20 minutes at 180º C, cooking 4 at a time.
4. Top with any burger toppings of your choice such as a fried egg, garnish and a delicious burger bun.
5. Serve and enjoy!!!

Chicken Milanese

Preparation Time: 5 minutes
Cooking Time: 14 minutes
Total Time: 19 minutes
Servings: 4
Ingredients:
- ½ Cup of panko
- ¼ Cup of grated parmesan cheese
- 4 Chicken breasts (boneless and skinless)
- Non-stick cooking spray

Sauce:
- 2 Tsp. of olive oil
- 2 Cups of grape tomatoes, cut in half
- 1 Shallot, peeled and diced
- 1 Tsp. of salt
- 1 Tsp. of pepper
- ½ Cup of fresh basil leaves
- ¼ Cup of red wine

Cooking Instructions:
1. In a small bowl, mix the panko and cheese together.
2. Spray your chicken with non-stick cooking spray and then dip it into the panko and cheese mixture and then coat with nonstick cooking spray.
3. Place in your Air-fryer pan, cook for 7 minutes at 390º C then flip it and cook for another 7 minutes. When the chicken is well cooked, make your sauce according to the following the steps below:
4. In a small saucepan combine the oil, heat until hot, then stir in the tomatoes, shallow, salt, and pepper, mix well.
5. Cook for about 5 minutes at 390º C then add the wine and heat up only about 35 seconds. Remove from heat and stir in the fresh basil. Spoon the sauce over the chicken.
6. Serve immediately and enjoy!!!

MAIN MEAL RECIPES

Inside Out Cheeseburgers

Preparation Time: 8 minutes
Cooking Time: 20 minutes
Total Time: 28 minutes
Servings: 2
Ingredients:
- 12 Oz (¾ pound) lean ground beef

- 3 Tbsp. minced onion
- 4 Tsp. ketchup
- 2 Tsp. yellow mustard
- Salt and freshly ground black pepper
- 4 Slices of Cheddar cheese, broken into smaller pieces
- 8 Hamburger dill pickle chips

Cooking Instructions:
1. Mix together the ground beef, minced onion, ketchup, mustard, salt and pepper in a large bowl. Divide the meat into four equal portions.
2. For the stuffed burgers, flatten each portion of meat into a thin patty. Add 4 pickle chips and half of the cheese onto the center of two of the patties, leaving a rim around the edge of the patty exposed.
3. Add the remaining two patties on top of the first, press the meat together and tightly seal the edges.
4. With the burgers on a flat surface, press the sides of the burger with the palm of your hand to create a straight edge.
5. This will help keep the stuffing inside the burger while it cooks. Pre-heat the Air Fryer to 370° F. Add the burgers inside Air Fryer basket and Air-fry for 20 minutes.
6. After 10 minutes of the cooking time, turn the burgers over to cook the other side. Top with lettuce and tomato.
7. Serve immediately!!!

Cauliflower Chickpea Tacos

Preparation Time: 10 minutes
Cooking Time: 20 minutes
Total Time: 30 minutes
Servings: 5

Cooking Ingredients:
- 4 Cups of cauliflower florets cut into bite-sized pieces
- 19 Oz. can of chickpeas drained and rinsed
- 2 Tbsp. olive oil
- 2 Tbsp. taco seasoning

Optional Toppings:
- 8 Small tortillas
- 2 Avocados sliced
- 4 Cups of cabbage shredded
- Coconut yogurt to drizzle

Cooking Instructions:
1. Pre-heat Air Fryer to 200° C.
2. In a large bowl, toss the cauliflower and chickpeas with the olive oil and taco seasoning.
3. Put everything into the basket of your Air Fryer. Cook in the Air Fryer for 20 minutes at 200° C. Cauliflower will be golden but not burnt.
4. Add your optional toppings like avocado slices, cabbage and coconut yogurt (or regular yogurt).
5. Serve and enjoy!!!

Roasted Vegetable Pasta Salad

Preparation Time: 10 minutes
Cooking Time: 15 minutes
Total Time: 25 minutes
Servings: 7
Ingredients:
- 1 Orange pepper, large chunks
- 1 Green pepper, large chunks
- 1 Red pepper, large chunks
- 1 Zucchini, sliced in half moons
- 1 Yellow squash, sliced in half moons
- 1 Red onion, sliced
- 4 Oz. brown mushrooms, halved
- Italian seasoning
- Salt and fresh ground black pepper
- 1 Lb. penne rigate or rigatoni, cooked
- 1 Cup of grape tomatoes, halved
- ½ Cup of pitted Kalamata olives, halved
- 3 Tbsp. balsamic vinegar
- ¼ Cup of olive oil
- 2 Tbsp. chopped fresh basil

Cooking Instructions:
1. Preheat the air fryer to 380º F.
2. Put the peppers, zucchini, yellow squash, red onion and mushrooms in a large bowl, drizzle with a little of the olive oil and toss to coat well. Add the Italian seasoning and season with salt and pepper.
3. Air-fry for 15 minutes at 380ºF or until the vegetables are soft. Shake the basket halfway during the cooking time to evenly roast vegetables.
4. Mix the cooked pasta, roasted vegetables, tomatoes and olives in a large bowl. Put the balsamic vinegar and toss. Add enough olive oil to coat everything nicely.
5. Season with salt and freshly ground black pepper to taste. Refrigerate the salad until you are ready to serve. Stir in the fresh basil right before serving.
6. Serve and enjoy!!!

Prosciutto, Spinach & Mushroom Pizza

Preparation Time: 20 minutes
Cooking Time: 35 minutes
Total Time: 55 minutes
Servings: 3
Ingredients:
- 3 Oz. button mushrooms, sliced

- ½ Cup of frozen spinach, thawed
- 1 Tbsp. olive oil
- ¼ Tsp. Italian seasoning
- 12 Oz. pizza dough
- ⅓ Cup of pizza sauce
- 1½ Cups of grated mozzarella cheese
- 3 Oz. thinly sliced prosciutto

Cooking Instructions:
1. Toss the mushrooms with the olive oil and Italian seasoning, and set aside to marinate for at least 15 minutes.
2. Squeeze as much liquid as possible from the spinach and set the spinach aside as well. Pre-heat Air Fryer to 370° F.
3. Grease the inside of Air Fryer pan with olive oil or use a pan with a non-stick surface. Roll or stretch the pizza dough out into a circle that is 8 to 9 inches in diameter.
4. Transfer it to the pan, pressing the crust up the sides of the pan. Dock the dough by piercing holes in the bottom crust with a fork.
5. Transfer the pan to the Air Fryer basket. Air-fry at 370° F for 5 minutes. Remove the pan from the air fryer.
6. Flip the crust over in the pan by inverting it onto a plate and sliding it back into the pan. Return the pan to the air fryer and Air-fry for 5 minutes to brown the bottom of the crust.
7. Flip the crust back over in the pan. Fill the inside of the pizza crust with the sauce and top with half of the mozzarella cheese. Layer half of the spinach and mushrooms over the cheese.
8. Repeat with another layer of cheese and another layer of spinach and mushrooms. Tear the prosciutto up into pieces and scatter the pieces on top of the pizza.
9. Return the pan to the Air Fryer. Cook at 350° F for 12 minutes until crust is brown and the cheese has melted.
10. Top with a nice salad and a glass of red wine. Serve and enjoy!!!

Stir Fried Zoodles and Vegetables with Tofu

Preparation Time: 20 minutes
Cooking Time: 30 minutes
Total Time: 50 minutes
Servings: 3

Ingredients:
- 1 Tbsp. canola oil
- 2 Tbsp. rice wine vinegar
- 2 Tbsp. brown rice syrup or honey
- 2 Tbsp. sriracha chili sauce
- 2 Tbsp. soy sauce
- 1 Tbsp. sesame oil

- 1 Tsp. minced fresh ginger
- 1 Lb. extra firm tofu, cubed
- ½ Onion, sliced
- 2 Carrots, sliced
- 1 Red bell pepper, sliced
- 1 Cup of snow peas, sliced lengthwise
- 1 Can baby corn, drained
- 8 Oz. spiralized zucchini (zoodles)
- Fresh cilantro leaves

Cooking Instructions:
1. In a small mixing bowl, mix together canola oil, rice wine vinegar, brown rice syrup, sriracha chili sauce, soy sauce, sesame oil, and ginger.
2. Add the tofu and let it marinate for 15 minutes. Pre-heat the Air Fryer to 400° F. Remove the tofu from the marinade with a slotted spoon and turn it to the Air Fryer basket. Reserve the marinade.
3. Air-fry the tofu at 400° F. for 15 minutes or until the tofu is nicely browned and crispy, shaking the basket a few times during the cooking process.
4. Remove it from the Air Fryer and set it aside. Put the onion and carrots to the Air Fryer and Air-fry at 400° F. for 5 minutes.
5. Put red pepper, snow peas, baby corn and continue to Air-fry for another 5 minutes. Toss in the zucchini and Air-fry for another 5 minutes, shaking the basket once during the cooking process.
6. Return the tofu to the Air Fryer basket with the vegetables and pour the reserved marinade over the top.
7. Toss everything to coat with the sauce. Air-fry for just a few more minutes until the vegetables are tender and heated through.
8. Turn everything to serving bowls and pour any marinade from the Air Fryer drawer on top. Top with a few fresh cilantro leaves.
9. Serve and enjoy!!!

General Tso's Cauliflower

Preparation Time: 10 minutes
Cooking Time: 25 minutes
Total Time: 35 minutes
Servings: 3

Ingredients:

- 1 Head cauliflower cut in florets
- ¾ Cup of all-purpose flour, divided
- 3 Eggs
- 1 Cup of panko breadcrumbs
- Canola or peanut oil, in a spray bottle
- 2 Tbsp. oyster sauce
- ¼ Cup of soy sauce
- 2 Tsp. chili paste
- 2 Tbsp. rice wine vinegar
- 2 Tbsp. sugar
- ¼ Cup of water
- White or brown rice for serving
- Steamed broccoli

Cooking Instructions:

1. Set up a dredging station using three bowls. Put the cauliflower in a large bowl and sprinkle ¼ cup of the flour over the top.
2. Put the eggs in a second bowl and combine the panko breadcrumbs and remaining ½ cup flour in a third bowl.
3. Toss the cauliflower in the flour to coat all the florets thoroughly. Dip the cauliflower florets in the eggs and finally toss them in breadcrumbs to coat on all sides.
4. Put the coated cauliflower florets on a baking sheet and spray generously with canola or peanut oil. Pre-heat the Air Fryer to 400° F.
5. Air-fry the cauliflower at 400° F for 15 minutes, flipping the florets over for the last 3 minutes of the cooking time and spray again with oil. While the cauliflower is air-frying, make the General Tso Sauce.
6. Mix the oyster sauce, soy sauce, chili paste, rice wine vinegar, sugar and water in a saucepan and bring the mixture to a boil on the stovetop.
7. Lower the heat and let it simmer for 10 minutes, stirring occasionally. When the timer is up on the Air Fryer, transfer the cauliflower to a large bowl.
8. Pour the sauce over it all and toss to coat. Make white or brown rice and some steamed broccoli to be available.
9. Serve and enjoy!!!

Quick Roasted Tomato Sauce with Capers and Basil

Preparation Time: 10 minutes
Cooking Time: 22 minutes
Total Time: 32 minutes
Servings: 2

Ingredients:
- 1½ Pints cherry tomatoes, halved
- 2 Tbsp. olive oil
- 1 Tbsp. white wine vinegar
- 1 Clove garlic, minced
- 1 Shallot, diced
- 2 Tbsp. capers
- 1 Tsp. Italian seasoning
- ½ Lb. dried pasta, cooked
- ¼ Cup of chopped fresh basil
- Grated Parmesan cheese, for serving

Cooking Instructions:
1. Pre-heat the air fryer to 400°F. Toss the cherry tomatoes, olive oil, white wine vinegar, garlic, shallots, capers, and Italian seasoning together in a bowl.
2. Season with salt and freshly ground black pepper. Turn the ingredients to the Air Fryer basket.
3. Air-fry for 20 minutes at 400° F shaking the basket several times during cooking time. Crush the tomatoes slightly.
4. Toss the hot pasta with the tomato sauce. Add the liquid from the bottom drawer of the Air Fryer to the pasta to loosen the sauce.
5. Stir in the fresh basil and season with salt and freshly ground black pepper to taste. Top with grated Parmesan cheese.
6. Serve and enjoy!!!

Curry Chickpeas

Preparation Time: 7 minutes
Cooking Time: 15 minutes
Total Time: 22 minutes
Servings: 4

Ingredients:
- 1 (15-oz.) Can no-salt-added chickpeas (garbanzo beans), drained and rinsed (about 1 ½ cups)
- 2 Tbsp. red wine vinegar
- 2 Tbsp. olive oil
- 2 Tsp. curry powder
- ½ Tsp. ground turmeric
- ¼ Tsp. ground coriander
- ¼ Tsp. ground cumin
- ¼ Tsp. plus
- 1/8 Tsp. ground cinnamon
- ¼ Tsp. kosher salt
- ½ Tsp. Aleppo pepper Thinly sliced fresh cilantro

Cooking Instructions:
1. Smash chickpeas gently with your hands in a medium bowl (do not crush); discard chickpea skins.
2. Add vinegar and oil to chickpeas, and toss to coat. Put curry powder, turmeric, coriander, cumin, and cinnamon; stir gently to mix properly.
3. Place chickpeas in single layer in Air Fryer basket, and cook at 400° F for about 15 minutes. Shake chickpeas regularly while it's still cooking.
4. Flip chickpeas onto a bowl. Sprinkle with salt, Aleppo pepper, and cilantro; toss to coat.
5. Serve immediately!!!

Chicken Wing Drumettes

Preparation Time: 15 minutes
Cooking Time: 30 minutes
Total Time: 45 minutes
Servings: 2

Ingredients:
- 10 Large chicken drumettes
- Cooking spray
- ¼ Cup of rice vinegar
- 3 Tbsp. honey
- 2 Tbsp. unsalted chicken stock
- 1 Tbsp. lower-sodium soy sauce
- 1 Tbsp. toasted sesame oil
- 3/8 Tsp. crushed red pepper
- 1 Garlic clove, finely chopped
- 2 Tbsp. chopped unsalted roasted peanuts
- 1 Tbsp. chopped fresh chives

Cooking Instructions:
1. Put chicken in single layer in Air Fryer basket; coat well with cooking spray. Cook at 400° F for about 30 minutes, Shake chickpeas regularly while it's still cooking.
2. Stir together vinegar, honey, stock, soy sauce, oil, crushed red pepper, and garlic in a small skillet.
3. Bring to a simmer over medium-high; cook until slightly thickened and almost syrupy, 6 minutes.
4. Place drumettes in a medium bowl. Add honey mixture, and toss to coat. Sprinkle with peanuts and chives.
5. Serve and enjoy!!!

Cauliflower Pan Pizza

Preparation Time: 10 minutes
Cooking Time: 20 minutes
Total Time: 30 minutes
Servings: 2

Ingredients:
- 2 Cups of "riced" or grated cauliflower (about ½ of large head)
- ⅓ Cup of Parmesan cheese
- 1½ Cups of grated mozzarella cheese, divided
- ½ Tsp. oregano
- 2 Tbsp. flour
- 1 Egg
- Salt
- Freshly ground black pepper
- ¼ Cup of pizza sauce
- Fresh basil leaves

Cooking Instructions:
1. Pre-heat the Air Fryer to 400°F. Grate the cauliflower with a box grater or finely chop it in a food processor.
2. Place the cauliflower in the center of a clean kitchen towel and twist it to squeeze all the water out.
3. Put the cauliflower in a large bowl and put the Parmesan cheese, ½ cup of the mozzarella cheese, oregano, flour, egg, salt and pepper. Mix properly.
4. Line the inside of Air Fryer baking pan with aluminum foil. Spread the cauliflower mixture into pan, pressing it up the sides of the pan.
5. Air-fry for 10 minutes. Remove the pan from air fryer and invert the cauliflower crust onto a plate. Flip over the crust in the baking pan to cook the bottom of the crust.
6. Air-fry at 400°F for 5 minutes. Remove the pan from Air Fryer and invert the crust back onto aluminum foil so that the crust is now right side up again.
7. Put the foil and crust back into the baking pan. Spread the pizza sauce over the crust and top with the remaining mozzarella cheese and some dried oregano.
8. Air-fry the pizza at 360°F for 5 minutes or until the cheese is melted and browned. Let the pizza sit in the Air Fryer for a few minutes after it has finished cooking.
9. Pull the pizza out of the pan with the aluminum foil and turn it to a cutting board. Remove the foil. Top the pizza with fresh basil, cut into four wedges.
10. Serve immediately and enjoy!!!

Jalapeno Poppers

Preparation Time: 10 minutes
Cooking Time: 8 minutes
Total Time: 18 minutes

Servings: 2

Ingredients:
- 10 Jalapeno peppers halved and deseeded
- 8 Oz. of cream cheese I used a dairy-free cream cheese
- ¼ C fresh parsley
- ¾ C gluten-free tortilla or bread crumbs

Cooking Instructions:
1. Mix together ½ of crumbs and cream cheese. When it is combined, add the parsley. Stuff each pepper with this mixture.
2. Gently press the tops of the peppers into the remaining ¼ C of crumbs to create the top coating.
3. Cook in Air Fryer at 370° F for 8 minutes.
4. Serve and enjoy!!!

Sticky Mushroom Rice

Preparation Time: 16 minutes
Cooking Time: 20 minutes
Total Time: 26 minutes
Servings: 6

Ingredients:

- 16 Oz. jasmine rice uncooked
- 1/2 Cup of soy sauce you can use gluten free tamari
- 4 Tbsp. maple syrup
- 4 Cloves garlic finely chopped
- 2 Tsp. Chinese 5 Spice
- 1/2 Tsp. ground ginger
- 4 Tbsp. white wine you can use rice vinegar
- 16 Oz. cremini mushrooms wiped clean, you can cut any huge mushrooms in half
- 1/2 Cup of peas frozen

Cooking Instructions:

1. You may begin to cook your rice first so that it will be done and hot at the same time as the sauce.
2. Mix the first 6 ingredients together and set aside.
3. Put the mushrooms in the Air Fryer. Cook in Air Fryer at 350º F for 10 minutes.
4. Open the Air Fryer, pull out the pot and shake.
5. Pour the liquid mixture and peas over the top of the mushrooms. Stir and cook for another 5 minutes.
6. Pour the mushroom and pea sauce over the pot of rice and stir.
7. Serve immediately and enjoy!!!

EGG RECIPES

Easy Cheese Omelette

Preparation Time: 5 minutes
Cooking Time: 8 minutes
Total Time: 13 minutes
Servings: 3

Ingredients:
- 2 Eggs, room temperature
- ¼ Cup of cream
- ¼ Cup of shredded cheddar cheese
- Salt and pepper to taste

Cooking Instructions:
1. In a small bowl, mix together the eggs, cream, salt, and pepper.
2. Pour the mixture into your Air Fryer pan and put the pan into the Air Fryer for 4 minutes at 350º F.
3. When the time is up, sprinkle your cheese on top and cook for another 4 minutes at 350º F.
4. Carefully remove your pan from the Air Fryer, and use a spatula to flip the omelet onto the pan.
5. Serve immediately and enjoy!!!

Southern Deviled Eggs

Preparation Time: 5 minutes
Cooking Time: 3 minutes
Total Time: 8 minutes
Servings: 3

Ingredients:
- 6 Eggs hardboiled
- 3 Tbsp. mayonnaise
- 1 ½ Tbsp. sweet pickle relish
- 1 Tsp. mustard
- Salt and pepper to taste
- Garnishing: paprika and sweet baby gherkin,

Cooking Instructions:
1. Boil the eggs and then place the eggs in ice water or in the refrigerator to cool.
2. Cut the eggs in half and scoop out the yolk, put them into a bowl. When you remove all of the yolks from the eggs, mash the yolks up, using a fork.
3. Add the mayonnaise, mustard, relish, salt, and pepper; and stir until well combined and smooth.
4. When the yolk mixture is smooth, add it to a piping bag and pipe it into the empty white shells.
5. Put a dash of paprika, and a slice of gherkin.
6. Serve and enjoy!!!

Hard Boiled Eggs

Preparation Time: 2 minutes
Cooking Time: 18 minutes
Total Time: 20 minutes
Servings: 3
Ingredients:
- 8 Eggs

Instructions:
1. Put the eggs in a bowl just to restrain them from rattling around.
2. Cook in Air Fryer at 260º F for 18 minutes.
3. When the timer is up, remove the bowl and put the eggs in cold water.
4. Wait a minute and then peel.
5. Serve immediately and enjoy!!!

Egg Benedict

Preparation Time: 15minutes
Cooking Time: 9 minutes
Total Time: 24 minutes
Servings: 4
Ingredients:
- 4 Piece Canadian Bacon or bacon
- 4 Eggs
- 2 English Muffin
- Hollandaise Sauce:
- 5 Tbsp. melted butter
- 3 Egg yolks
- 1 Tbsp. lemon juice
- Salt and pepper to taste

Cooking Instructions:
1. Cut your Canadian bacon out with a biscuit or cookie cutter.
2. Spray your ramekin with non-stick cooking spray and then crack an egg into the ramekin.
3. Put them in your Air Fryer at 320º F for 3 minutes. Check on them, and flip over the other side of the bacon. If your egg is done, remove it.
4. Otherwise, set it for another 3 minutes. When the egg and bacon are done, remove it and put your English muffin in the Air Fryer.
5. Set the temperature to 365º F for 3 minutes. Remove your English muffin. For the sauce, put the egg yolks, lemon juice and melted butter in a blender. Mix until well combined.
6. Flip onto a serving plate (English muffin on the bottom, then the piece of Canadian bacon, and then the baked egg on top, and then pour the sauce over it).
7. Garnish with some parsley.
8. Serve and enjoy!!!

Baked Eggs

Preparation Time: 5 minutes
Cooking Time: 5 minutes
Total Time: 10 minutes
Servings: 3
Ingredients:
- 3 Eggs
- Non-stick cooking spray
- Seasonings

Cooking Instructions:
1. Preheat your Air Fryer to 180º F.
2. Generously spray your ramekin and then crack the eggs into your ramekin.
3. Season as you wish (You can use salt and pepper).
4. Bake in Air Fryer for 5 minutes at 330º F.
5. Serve and enjoy!!!

Thai Peanut Chicken Egg Rolls

Preparation Time: 10 minutes
Cooking Time: 8 minutes
Total Time: 18 minutes
Servings: 4 egg rolls
- **Ingredients:**
- 4 Egg roll wrappers
- 2 C. rotisserie chicken, shredded
- ¼ C. Thai peanut sauce
- 1 Medium carrot, very thinly sliced or rib boned
- 3 Green onions, chopped
- ¼ Red bell pepper, julienned
- Non-stick cooking spray or sesame oil

Cooking Instructions:
1. Preheat Air Fryer to 390° F.
2. In a small bowl, toss the chicken with the Thai peanut sauce. Place the egg roll wrappers on a clean dry surface.
3. Over the bottom third of an egg roll wrapper, arrange ¼ the carrot, bell pepper and onions. Spoon ½ cup of the chicken mixture over the vegetables.
4. Moisten the outside edges of the wrapper with water. Fold the sides of the wrapper toward the center and roll tightly. Repeat with remaining wrappers.
5. Spray the assembled egg rolls with non-stick cooking spray. Flip them over and spray the back sides as well.
6. Place the egg rolls in the Air Fryer and bake at 390° F for 8 minutes or until they are crispy and golden brown.
7. Slice in half and flip onto serving plates with additional Thai Peanut Sauce for dipping.
8. Serve and enjoy!!!

Scrambled Eggs

Preparation Time: 1 minute
Cooking Time: 9 minutes
Total Time: 10 minutes
Servings: 2
Calories: 197 kcal
Ingredients:
- 2 Slices Whole meal Bread
- 4 Large Eggs

- Salt & Pepper

Cooking Instructions:
1. Warm up your bread at for 3 minutes so that it is harder like toast.
2. Crack your eggs into your Air Fryer and give them a quick stir. Add the seasoning and put the baking pan inside the Air Fryer.
3. Cook for 2 minutes at 200º C. Stir and cook for another 4 minutes at the same temperature.
4. Pour the scrambled eggs over the whole meal toast.
5. Serve and enjoy!!!

Egg in Hole

Preparation Time: 5 minutes
Cooking Time: 10 minutes
Total Time: 15 minutes
Servings: 1

Ingredients:
- 1 Piece of toast
- 1 Egg
- Salt and pepper

Cooking Instructions:
1. Spray your Air Fryer safe pan with non-stick cooking spray.
2. Put your piece of bread into your Air Fryer safe pan.
3. Make a hole with a cup or cookie cutter and remove the bread. Crack the egg into the hole.
4. Air Fry at 330º F for 6 minutes. Use a spatula to flip the egg and Air Fry another 4 minutes.
5. Serve and enjoy!!!

FISH & SEAFOOD RECIPES

Steamed Mussels

Preparation Time: 5 minutes
Cooking Time: 5 minutes
Total Time: 10 minutes
Servings: 3
Ingredients:
- 1 Lb. mussels
- 1 Tbsp. butter
- 1 Cup of water
- 2 Tsp. minced garlic
- 1 Tsp. chives
- 1 Tsp. basil
- 1 Tsp. parsley

Cooking Instructions:
1. Pre-heat your Air Fryer to 390º F.
2. Soak your mussel for 30 minutes, use a brush and clean your mussels, and remove the "beard".
3. In your Air Fryer safe pan, add the water, butter, garlic, chives, basil, parsley, and mussels.
4. Air fry for 3 minutes at 390º F, check and see if they are opened. If they are not opened, cook for another 2 minutes.
5. Once all of the mussels are opened, they are ready for eating. Note: Time depends on the wattage of your Air Fryer and the number of mussels.
6. Just keep on checking, you don't have to make them overcooked. Immediately they are opened, they are cooked and ready for eating.
7. Serve and enjoy!!!

Roasted Salmon with Fennel Salad

Preparation Time: 15 minutes
Cooking Time: 10 minutes
Total Time: 25 minutes
Servings: 4

Ingredients:
- 2 Tsp. finely chopped fresh flat-leaf parsley
- 1 Tsp. finely chopped fresh thyme
- 1 Tsp. kosher salt, divided
- 4 (6-oz.) Skinless center-cut salmon fillets
- 2 Tbsp. olive oil
- 4 Cups of thinly sliced fennel (from 2 [15-oz.] heads fennel)
- 2/3 Cup of 2% reduced-fat Greek yogurt
- 1 Garlic clove, grated
- 2 Tbsp. fresh orange juice (from 1 orange)
- 1 Tsp. fresh lemon juice (from 1 lemon)
- 2 Tbsp. chopped fresh dill

Cooking Instructions:
1. Mix together parsley, thyme, and ½ tsp. of the salt in a small bowl. Brush salmon with oil.
2. Sprinkle evenly with herb mixture. Add 2 salmon fillets in Air Fryer basket, and cook at 350°F for 10 minutes or until desired degree of doneness.
3. Transfer to preheated oven to keep warm. Repeat procedure with remaining fillets.
4. While salmon cooks, toss together fennel, yogurt, garlic, orange juice, lemon juice, dill, and remaining ½ tsp. salt in a medium bowl. Garnish with fennel salad.
5. Serve and enjoy!!!

Spicy Fish Street Tacos with Sriracha Slaw

Preparation Time: 15 minutes
Cooking Time: 5 minutes
Total Time: 20 minutes
Servings: 3

Ingredients:
Sriracha Slaw:
- ½ Cup of mayonnaise
- 2 Tbsp. rice vinegar
- 1 Tsp. sugar
- 2 Tbsp. sriracha chili sauce
- 5 Cups of shredded green cabbage
- ¼ Cup of shredded carrots
- 2 Scallions, chopped
- Salt and freshly ground black pepper

Tacos:
- ½ Cup of flour
- 1 Tsp. chili powder
- ½ Tsp. ground cumin
- 1 Tsp. salt
- Freshly ground black pepper
- ½ Tsp. baking powder
- 1 Egg, beaten
- ¼ Cup of milk
- 1 Cup of breadcrumbs
- 12 Oz. mahi-mahi or snapper fillets
- 1 Tbsp. canola or vegetable oil
- 6 (6-inch) Flour tortillas
- 1 Lime, cut into wedges

Cooking Instructions:
1. Mix the mayonnaise, rice vinegar, sugar, and sriracha sauce in a large bowl. Mix well and add the green cabbage, carrots, and scallions.
2. Toss until all the vegetables are coated with the dressing and season with salt and pepper. Refrigerate the slaw until you are ready to serve the tacos.
3. Mix the flour, chili powder, cumin, salt, pepper and baking powder in a bowl. Put the egg and milk. Mix until the batter is smooth. Place the breadcrumbs in shallow dish.
4. Cut the fish fillets into 1-inch wide sticks, approximately 4-inches long. You should have about 12 fish sticks total. Dip the fish sticks into the batter, coating all sides.
5. Let the excess batter drip off the fish and then roll them in the breadcrumbs, patting the crumbs onto all sides of the fish sticks.
6. Set the coated fish on a plate or baking sheet until all the fish has been coated. Pre-heat the Air Fryer to 400° F. Spray the coated fish sticks with oil on all sides.

7. Spray or brush the inside of the air fryer basket with oil and transfer the fish to the basket. Put as many sticks as you can in one layer, leaving a little room around each stick.
8. Place any remaining sticks on top perpendicular to the first layer. Air-fry the fish for 3 minutes at 400º F. turn the fish sticks over and Air Fry for another 2 minutes.
9. While the fish is Air-frying, warm the tortillas shells at 350º F. Fold the tortillas in half and keep them warm until the remaining tortillas and fish are ready.
10. To assemble the tacos, put two pieces of the fish in each tortilla shell and top with the sriracha slaw. Squeeze the lime wedge over top and dig in.
11. Serve and enjoy!!!

Sockeye Salmon enPapillote with Potatoes, Fennel and Dill

Preparation Time: 10 minutes
Cooking Time: 20 minutes
Total Time: 30 minutes
Servings: 2

Ingredients:
- 3 Fingerling potatoes, thinly sliced ¼-inch thick
- ½ Bulb fennel, thinly sliced ¼-inch thick
- 4 Tbsp. butter, melted
- Salt and freshly ground black pepper
- Fresh dill
- 2 (6 oz.) Sockeye salmon fillets
- 8 Cherry tomatoes, halved
- ¼ Cup of dry vermouth (or white wine or fish stock)

Cooking Instructions:
1. Pre-heat the Air Fryer to 400°F. Boil a small saucepan of salted water. Blanch the potato slices for 2 minutes or until they just start to soften slightly.
2. Drain and dry with a clean kitchen towel. Cut out 2 large rectangles of parchment paper (about 13" by 15" each).
3. Toss the potatoes, fennel, half of the melted butter, salt and freshly ground black pepper together in a bowl. Divide the vegetables between the two pieces of parchment paper, placing the vegetables on one half of each rectangle.
4. Sprinkle some fresh dill on top. Put a fillet of salmon on each pile of vegetables. Season the fish very well with salt and pepper.
5. Toss the cherry tomatoes on top. Drizzle the remaining butter over the fish. Divide the vermouth between the two packages, drizzling it over the fish.
6. Fold up each parchment square by first folding the rectangles in half over the fish. Starting at one corner, make a series of straight folds on the outer rim of the squares to seal the edge together.
7. Put the two packages onto a baking sheet and bake at 400ºF for 20 minutes. The package should be puffed up and slightly browned when fully cooked.
8. Serve and enjoy!!!

Lemon-Dill Salmon Burgers

Preparation Time: 10 minutes
Cooking Time: 8 minutes
Total Time: 18 minutes
Servings: 4

Ingredients:
- 2 (6 Oz.) Fillets of salmon, finely chopped by hand or in a food processor
- 1 Cup of fine breadcrumbs

- 1 Tsp. freshly grated lemon zest
- 2 Tbsp. chopped fresh dill weed
- 1 Tsp. salt
- Freshly ground black pepper
- 2 Eggs, lightly beaten

Cooking Instructions:
1. Pre-heat the Air Fryer to 400°F.
2. Mix together all the ingredients in a bowl and divide into four balls. Flatten the balls into patties, making an indentation in the center of each patty with your thumb.
3. Flatten the sides of the burgers so that they fit nicely into the Air Fryer basket. Turn the burgers into the Air Fryer basket and Air-fry for 4 minutes.
4. Flip the burgers over and Air-fry for another 4 minutes or until nicely browned.
5. Top with lettuce, tomato, red onion, avocado, mayonnaise or mustard.
6. Serve and enjoy!!!

Parmesan Shrimp

Preparation Time: 8 minutes
Cooking Time: 10 minutes
Total Time: 18 minutes
Servings: 2

Ingredients:
- 2 Lbs. jumbo cooked shrimp, peeled and deveined
- 4 Cloves garlic, minced
- 2/3 Cup of parmesan cheese, grated
- 1 Tsp. pepper
- 1/2 Tsp. oregano
- 1 Tsp. basil
- 1 Tsp. onion powder
- 2 Tbsp. olive oil
- Lemon, quartered

Cooking Instructions:
- In a large bowl, mix together garlic, parmesan cheese, pepper, oregano, basil, onion powder and olive oil.
- Carefully toss shrimp in the mixture until evenly-coated.
- Spray Air Fryer basket with non-stick spray and place shrimp in basket.
- Cook at 350º F for 10 minutes or until seasoning on shrimp is browned.
- Squeeze the lemon over the shrimp.
- Serve immediately and enjoy!!!

Lobster Tails

Preparation Time: 10 minutes
Cooking Time: 6 minutes
Total Time: 16 minutes
Servings: 2

Ingredients:
- 4 Lobster tails
- 2 Tbsp. of melted butter
- ½ Tsp. of salt
- 1 Tsp. of pepper

Cooking Instructions:

1. Pre-heat the Air Fryer to 380º F. Melt the butter.
2. Cut the lobster with kitchen scissors, right through the tail section and then break the shell and pull back the shell with your fingers.
3. Brush your lobster tails with butter, add some salt and pepper, then Air-fry at 380º F for 4 minutes.
4. Add the melted butter and Air-fry for another 2 minutes. Top with additional butter.
5. Serve and enjoy!!!

Bang Bang Fried Shrimp

Preparation Time: 10 minutes
Cooking Time: 20 minutes
Total Time: 30 minutes
Servings: 4

Ingredients:
- 1 Lb. raw shrimp peeled and deveined
- 1 Egg white 3 tbsp.
- ½ Cup of all-purpose flour
- ¾ Cup of panko bread crumbs
- 1 Tsp paprika
- McCormick's Grill Mates Montreal Chicken Seasoning to taste
- Salt and pepper to taste
- Cooking spray

Bang Bang Sauce:
- ⅓ Cup of plain, non-fat Greek yogurt
- 2 Tbsp. sriracha
- ¼ Cup of sweet chili sauce

Cooking Instructions:
1. Pre-heat Air Fryer to 400º F. Season the shrimp with the seasonings. Put the flour, egg whites, and panko bread crumbs in three separate bowls.
2. Dip the shrimp in the flour, the egg whites and the panko bread crumbs last Just do a light dab so that most of the flour stays on the shrimp.
3. You want the egg white to adhere to the panko crumbs. Spray the shrimp with cooking spray. Do not spray directly on the shrimp.
4. The panko will go flying. Keep a little distance. Add the shrimp to the Air Fryer basket. Cook for 4 minutes at 400º F.
5. Open the basket and flip the shrimp to the other side. Cook for another 4 minutes or until crisp. For the Bang Bang Sauce, mix all of the ingredients in a small bowl. Mix thoroughly to combine.
6. Serve and enjoy!!!

Coconut Shrimp with Spicy Marmalade Sauce

Preparation Time: 10 minutes
Cooking Time: 20 minutes
Total Time: 30 minutes
Servings: 2
Calories: 620 kcal

Ingredients:
- 8 Large shrimp shelled and deveined
- 8 Oz. coconut milk

- ½ Cup of shredded sweetened coconut
- ½ Cup of panko bread
- ½ Tsp. cayenne pepper
- ¼ Tsp. kosher salt
- ¼ Tsp. fresh ground pepper
- ½ Cup of orange marmalade
- 1 Tbsp. honey
- 1 Tsp. mustard
- ¼ Tsp. hot sauce

Cooking Instructions:
1. Start by cleaning the shrimp and set aside.
2. Whisk together the coconut milk and season with salt and pepper in a small bowl and set aside.
3. Using another small bowl, whisk together the coconut, panko, cayenne pepper, salt and pepper.
4. Put the shrimp inside the coconut milk, the panko, one at a time and then put in the basket of your Air Fryer.
5. Repeat this step until all the shrimp are coated. Cook the shrimp in the Air Fryer for 20 minutes at 350º F.
6. Whisk together the marmalade, honey, mustard and hot sauce while the shrimp are cooking.
7. Serve immediately and enjoy!!!

Air Fryer Steak

Preparation Time: 2 minutes
Cooking Time: 12 minutes
Total Time: 14 minutes
Servings: 1

Ingredients:
- 1 New York Strip steak

Cooking Instructions:
1. Preheat your Air Fryer at 400º F for 5 minutes.
2. Put the steak in your Air Fryer and season it with seasoning of choice.
3. Cook in the Air Fryer at 400º F for 12 minutes and flip the steak at 6th or 7th minutes. Garnish with vegetables or mashed cauliflower.
4. Serve and enjoy!!!

Homemade Salmon Patties

Preparation Time: 5 minutes
Cooking Time: 10 minutes
Total Time: 15 minutes
Servings: 2

Ingredients:
- 14.75 Ounces salmon (I used pink)
- 1 Egg
- ¼ Cup of diced onion
- ½ Cup of bread crumbs
- 1 Tsp. dill weed

Cooking Instructions:
1. Prepare the fish by cleaning it, remove the bones and skin. Drain it.
2. In a small bowl, mix the egg, onion, dill weed, and breadcrumbs into the salmon.
3. Shape into patties and put them in the Air Fryer.
4. Cook in the Air Fryer at 370º F for 5 minutes. Turn them over and cook the other side and Air Fry for another 5 minutes.
5. Serve and enjoy!!!

Maryland Jumbo Lump Crab Cakes

Preparation Time: 5 minutes
Cooking Time: 15 minutes
Total Time: 20 minutes
Servings: 2

Ingredients:
- 1 Egg
- 2 Tbsp. mayonnaise
- 1 Onion peeled and diced
- 1/2 Tsp. Dijon mustard
- 1 Tsp. Worcestershire sauce
- 1 Tsp. Old Bay seasoning.
- ½ Tsp salt
- 2 Tbsp. fresh parsley diced
- 1 Cup of fresh crab meat
- 1 Cup of saltines crushed
- ½ Cup of panko

Cooking Instructions:
1. In a small mixing bowl, mix together the egg, mayonnaise, onion, Dijon mustard, Worcestershire, Old Bay seasoning, saltines, salt, and parsley.
2. Add the crab and mix carefully. Cut and shape the crab mixture into patties and dip them into the panko.
3. Coat both sides and put in the refrigerator for about an hour. Spray the crab cakes on both sides.
4. Add them in your Air Fryer basket and Air-fry at 350º F for 15 minutes.
5. Serve immediately and enjoy!!!

Easiest Breaded Shrimp

Preparation Time: 10 minutes
Cooking Time: 20 minutes
Total Time: 30 minutes
Servings: 2

Ingredients:
- 1 Lb. of shrimp, peeled and deveined
- 2 Eggs
- ½ Cup of panko
- ½ Cup of onion, peeled and diced
- 1 Tsp. of ginger
- 1 Tsp. of garlic powder
- 1 Tsp. of black pepper

Cooking Instructions:
1. Preheat your air fryer to 350º F.
2. In a small bowl, beat the eggs. In another bowl put the panko, onions, and spices.
3. Dip the shrimp in the egg and the panko bowl.
4. Air-fry at 350º F for 10 minutes. Turn to the other side and Air-fryer for another 10 minutes.
5. Serve and enjoy!!!

BLT Bites

Preparation Time: 10 minutes
Total Time: 10 minutes
Servings: 2

Ingredients:
- 20 Cherry tomatoes
- 1 Lb. sliced bacon, cooked and crumbled
- ½ Cup of mayonnaise
- 1/3 Cup of chopped green onions
- 3 Tbsp. grated Parmesan cheese
- 2 Tbsp. snipped fresh parsley

Cooking Instructions:
1. Make a little cut on top of each tomato.
2. Scoop out and discard pulp. Invert the tomatoes on a paper towel to drain.
3. Mix the remaining ingredients in a small bowl.
4. Spoon into tomatoes. Refrigerate for some hours.
5. Serve and enjoy!!!

Cajun French Fries

Preparation Time: 18 minutes
Cooking Time: 15 minutes
Total Time: 33 minutes
Servings: 2
Calories: 206 kcal

Ingredients:
- 568g White Potatoes peeled into chips
- 2.5ml Olive Oil
- 1 Tbsp. Cajun Spice
- 2 Tsp. Mexican Seasoning
- 1 Tsp. Mixed Spice
- 1 Tsp. Coriander
- Salt and Pepper

Cooking Instructions:
1. Put your peeled potatoes into a medium bowl.
2. Add cold water and soak in the fridge for 15 minutes.
3. After 15 minutes drain and remove all excess water as well as patting the potatoes dry.
4. Carefully season the potatoes. Put the olive oil and mix with your hands until your French Fries are well coated.
5. Put the French Fries in the Air Fryer and cook for 10 minutes at 320º F.
6. Flip over and cook for another 5 minutes at 400º F.
7. Serve and enjoy!!!

Bacon Wrapped Shrimp

Preparation Time: 2 minutes
Cooking Time: 7 minutes
Total Time: 9 minutes
Servings: 2

Ingredients:
- 16 Shrimp, cleaned and deveined
- 16 Slices of bacon

Cooking Instructions:
1. Preheat your Air Fryer to 390º F. Wrap every shrimp in bacon.
2. Put the prepared shrimp in the refrigerator for about 30 minutes.
3. Put them in the Air Fryer basket for about 5 minutes.
4. Flip them over and bake for another 2 minutes.
5. Serve and enjoy!!!

PORK & BEEF RECIPES

BBQ Ribs

Preparation Time: 1 minute
Cooking Time: 17 minutes
Total Time: 18 minutes
Servings: 2

Ingredients:
- 3 Lbs. baby back ribs
- 32 Oz. BBQ sauce (any type)
- Salt and pepper

Cooking Instructions:
1. Preheat your Air Fryer to 390º F. Season the ribs with salt, pepper and other spices that you have. Remove the membrane.
2. Dip your ribs into BBQ sauce and put them in your Air Fryer basket.
3. Air-fry at 390º F for 10 minutes. Turn to the other side and Air-fryer for another 7 minutes.
4. Remove from Air Fryer, add some extra sauce if you wish.
5. Serve and enjoy!!!

Honey Mustard Pork Chops

Preparation Time: 5 minutes
Cooking Time: 8 minutes
Total Time: 13 minutes
Servings: 4

Ingredients:
- 4 Pork chops ½ inch thick
- 4 Tbsp. mustard
- 2 Tbsp. honey
- 2 Tbsp. minced garlic
- 1 Tsp. salt
- 1 Tsp. pepper
- Oil to spray chops

Cooking Instructions:
1. In a large mixing bowl, mix together mustard, honey, garlic, salt, and pepper, pork chops and toss to coat with the sauce.
2. Spray the Air Fryer basket. Place the chops into the greased basket.
3. Air-fry at 350º F for 10 minutes. Flip to the other side, spray with oil and Air-fryer for another 2 minutes.
4. Serve and enjoy!!!

Beef Stir Fry with Homemade Marinade

Preparation Time: 10 minutes
Cooking Time: 13 minutes
Total Time: 23 minutes
Servings: 2

Ingredients:
- 1 Lb. of beef sirloin, cut into 2 inch strips
- 1½ Lb. of broccoli florets
- 1 Red pepper, cut into strips
- 1 Green pepper, cut into strips
- 1 Yellow pepper, cut into strips
- ½ Cup of onion, cut into strips
- ½ Cup of red onion, cut into strips

Sauce and Marinade:
- ¼ Cup of hoisin sauce
- 2 Tsp. of minced garlic
- 1 Tsp. of sesame oil
- 1 Tbsp. of soy sauce
- 1 Tsp. of ground ginger
- ¼ Cup of water

Cooking Instructions:
1. Put all of the ingredients for the sauce (marinate) including the meat into a bowl. Put in the refrigerator for about 20 minutes.
2. Put one tbsp. of oil and mix it in with the vegetables. Put your vegetables in the air fryer basket, and cook them at 200º F for 5 minutes.
3. Open the Air Fryer, stir the vegetables and make sure they are softened. You may cook for another 2 minutes if they are not softened.
4. Remove the vegetables and put them in a bowl. Put your meat into the Air Fryer basket and cook at 360º F for 4 minutes.
5. Flip to the other side, Air-fryer for another 2 minutes. Make your white rice available, top with the vegetables and meat.
6. Serve and enjoy!!!

Southern Style Fried Pork Chops

Preparation Time: 5 minutes
Cooking Time: 20 minutes
Total Time: 25 minutes
Servings: 4
Calories 173 kcal

Ingredients:
- 4 Pork chops (bone-in or boneless)
- 3 Tbsp. buttermilk
- 1/4 Cup all-purpose flour
- Salt to taste
- Pepper to taste
- 1 Ziploc bag
- Cooking oil spray

Cooking Instructions:
1. Carefully wash and pat dry the pork chops.
2. Season the pork chops with the seasoning salt and pepper.
3. Put the buttermilk over the pork chops, put the pork chops in a Ziploc bag with the flour and shake to fully coat.
4. Put the pork chops in the Air Fryer in layers. Spray the pork chops with cooking oil.
5. Air-fry at 380º F for 10 minutes. Flip over to the other side and Air-fryer for another 5 minutes.
6. Serve and enjoy!!!

Beef Hotpot

Preparation Time: 5 minutes
Cooking Time: 19 minutes
Total Time: 24 minutes
Servings: 4
Calories: 158 kcal

Ingredients:
- Leftover Stew
- 4 Large Carrots
- 4 Medium Potatoes
- Beef Gravy Granules
- 1 Tsp. Olive Oil
- Salt and Pepper

Cooking Instructions:
1. Peel and dice your carrots and place them into the bottom of your Instant Pot Pressure Cooker.
2. Add 250ml of warm water. Close and lock the lid in place. Cook on Manual High Pressure for 4 minutes. Peel your potatoes and thinly dice them into equal sizes.
3. Put salt, pepper and a tsp. of olive oil. Cook in the Air Fryer at 320º F for 10 minutes. Flip over to the other side and Air-fryer for another 5 minutes at 400º F.
4. When the Instant Pot beeps, do a manual pressure release, put your stew leftovers to your Instant Pot and stir well.
5. Put the beef gravy granules and using the sauté setting, stir until you have a thick liquid among your leftovers.
6. Place the filling in the bottom of your dishes, followed by your Air-fried potatoes on top.
7. Serve immediately!!!

Crispy Breaded Pork Chops

Preparation Time: 5 minutes
Cooking Time: 12 minutes
Total Time: 17 minutes
Servings: 2
Ingredients:
- Olive oil spray
- 6 (3/4-inch thick) Center cut boneless pork chops, fat trimmed (5 oz. each)
- Kosher salt
- 1 Large egg, beaten
- ½ Cup of panko crumbs
- 1/3 Cup of crushed cornflakes crumbs
- 2 Tbsp. grated parmesan cheese
- 1 ¼ Tsp. sweet paprika
- ½ Tsp. garlic powder
- ½ Tsp. onion powder
- ¼ Tsp. chili powder
- 1/8 Tsp. black pepper

Cooking Instructions:
1. Preheat the Air Fryer to 400° F for 12 minutes and lightly spray the basket with oil.
2. Season pork chops on both sides with ½ tsp kosher salt. In a large bowl, mix together the panko, cornflake crumbs and parmesan cheese.
3. Add 3/4 tsp. kosher salt, paprika, garlic powder, onion powder, chili powder and black pepper.
4. Put the beaten egg in another bowl. Dip the pork into the egg and crumb mixture.
5. Put 3 of the chops into the prepared Air Fryer basket and spray the top with oil.
6. Cook in the Air Fryer at 390° F for 12 minutes. Flip over to the other side and Air-fryer for another 5 minutes.
7. Repeat the same steps on the remaining chops.
8. Serve and enjoy!!!

Mongolian Beef

Preparation Time: 20 minutes
Cooking Time: 20 minutes
Total Time: 40 minutes
Servings: 4
Ingredients:
Meat:
- 1 Lb. Flank Steak

- ¼ Cup of Corn Starch

Sauce:
- 2 Tsp. Vegetable Oil
- ½ Tsp. Ginger
- 1 Tbsp. Minced Garlic
- ½ Cup of Soy Sauce or Gluten Free Soy Sauce
- ½ Cup of Water
- ¾ Cup of Brown Sugar Packed

Optional: Cooked Rice, green Beans and green Onions

Cooking Instructions:
1. Slice the steak in long pieces and then coat with the corn starch.
2. Add in the Air Fryer and cook at 390º F for 10 minutes on each side. Warm up all sauce ingredients in a medium sized saucepan on medium-high heat.
3. Whisk together the ingredients until it gets to a low boil. Once both the steak and sauce are cooked, place the steak in a bowl with the sauce.
4. Allow it soak in for about 8-10 minutes. Use tongs to remove the steak and let the excess sauce drip off.
5. Place steak on cooked rice and green beans, top with additional sauce of your choice.
6. Serve and enjoy!!!

Crispy Breaded Pork Chops

Preparation Time: 7 minutes
Cooking Time: 12 minutes
Total Time: 19 minutes
Servings: 3

Ingredients:
- Kosher salt
- ¼ Tsp. chili powder
- 1/8 Tsp. black pepper
- 6 (3/4 inch thick) center cut boneless pork chops, fat trimmed (5 oz. each)
- ½ Tsp. onion powder
- 1 Large egg, beaten
- ½ Cup of panko crumbs
- 1/3 Cup of crushed cornflakes crumbs
- Olive oil spray
- 2 Tbsp. grated parmesan cheese
- 1 ¼ Tsp. sweet paprika
- ½ Tsp. garlic powder

Cooking Instructions:
1. Pre-heat the Air Fryer to 400° F for 12 minutes. Sprinkle the basket with oil and season pork chops on both sides with ½ tsp. kosher salt.
2. In a large mixing bowl, mix together, cornflake crumbs, black pepper, parmesan cheese, 3/4 tsp kosher salt, paprika, garlic powder, panko, onion powder, chili powder.
3. In another small mixing bowl, put the beaten egg, dip the pork into the egg and then crumb mixture. Add 3 of the chops into the prepared basket and sprinkle with oil.
4. Cook in the Air Fryer at 400° F for 12 minutes. Flip over to the other side and Air-fryer for another 2 minutes.
5. Repeat the same steps on the remaining chops spraying oil on both sides.
6. Serve and enjoy!!!

Roast Beef

Preparation Time: 5 minutes
Cooking Time: 45 minutes
Total Time: 50 minutes
Servings: 6
Calories 320 kcal

Ingredients:
- 1 Tbsp. olive oil
- 1 Tsp. rosemary
- 2 Lbs. beef roast
- 1 Tsp. salt

Cooking Instructions:
1. Pre-heat Air Fryer to 360° F. In a small mixing bowl, mix together Olive oil, rosemary and sea salt.
2. Put beef in the mixture and turn to enable oil mixture to coat outside.
3. Put beef in Air Fryer basket and cook at 380° F for 45 minutes. Flip over to the other side and Air-fryer for another 5 minutes.
4. Remove roast beef from Air Fryer, cover with kitchen foil and leave to rest for about 10 minutes.
5. Serve and enjoy!!!

Sausage Rolls

Preparation Time: 5 minutes
Cooking Time: 10 minutes
Total Time: 15 minutes
Servings: 4
Calories: 149 kcal

Ingredients:
- 200g Minced Pork
- 1 Small Egg Beaten
- 2 ½ Weight Watchers Wraps
- Salt and Pepper
- 2 Tsp. Thyme

Cooking Instructions:
1. In a small bowl, mix together minced pork with the seasonings.
2. Prepare it to be in the shape of a sausage meat roll and put in a refrigerator for 10 minutes.
3. Put Weight Watchers Wrap onto a flat surface that is clean. Beat the egg and use it to brush the weight watchers.
4. Unlike a Swiss roll, place them in the Air Fryer basket in the center. Use egg to cover it up.
5. Cook at 400° F for 5 minutes on each side in the Air Fryer.
6. Serve immediately and enjoy!!!

Beef Empanadas

Preparation Time: 10 minutes
Cooking Time: 16 minutes
Total Time: 26 minutes
Servings: 8

Ingredients:
- 1 Egg white, whisked
- 8 Goya empanada discs (in frozen section), thawed
- 1 Tsp. water
- 1 Cup of picadillo

Cooking Instructions:
1. Pre-heat the Air Fryer to 325º F for 8 minutes.
2. Spray the basket with oil. In the center of each disc, put 2 tbsp. of picadillo.
3. Fold in half and seal the edges with fork. Do this to the remaining dough.
4. Whisk the egg whites with water and brush the tops of the empanadas.
5. Bake 3 at a time in the Air Fryer at 325º F for 8 minutes, or until golden. Remove from heat and do the same with the remaining empanadas.
6. Serve and enjoy!!!

SIDE DISH RECIPES

Cheese and Onion Pasties

Preparation Time: 5 minutes
Cooking Time: 12 minutes
Total Time: 17 minutes
Servings: 8
Calories: 92 kcal
Ingredients:
- 80g Diet Cheddar Cheese
- 1 Tbsp. Chives
- 60g Cheshire Cheese
- 4 Weight Watchers Wraps
- 2 Large Potatoes
- Salt and Pepper
- 1 Small White Onion
- 1 Small Egg Beaten

Cooking Instructions:
1. Peel and chop potatoes and onion. Put it in the Instant Pot Pressure Cooker.
2. Add a cup of water (250ml). Cover the lid on the Instant Pot, set the valve to sealing position and cook for 8 minutes.
3. Grate your cheese and slice your wraps in half while they are steaming. When the timer beeps, manually release pressure.
4. Drain the potatoes, onion and place back in the inner pot of Instant Pot. Put the seasoning and the grated cheese to the Instant Pot and mix thoroughly.
5. Put ½ a wrap at a time into the pasty press and brush with egg. Add pasty filling to one side but do not over fill it.
6. Create a pasty shape by pressing it down. Brush with egg on the outside.
7. Put in the Air Fryer and cook at 400º F for 2 minutes on each side.
8. Serve immediately and enjoy!!!

Brussels' Sprouts with Bacon

Preparation Time: 3 minutes
Cooking Time: 15 minutes
Total Time: 18 minutes
Servings: 2
Calories: 187 kcal
Ingredients:
- 4 Slices Back Bacon
- 450g Brussels' Sprouts

- Salt and Pepper

Cooking Instructions:
1. Cut out the core and the outside skin of the Brussels' Sprouts.
2. Put them into your Air Fryer and cook at 360º F for 10 minutes.
3. Dice your bacon while the Brussels' Sprouts are cooking.
4. Cut all the fatty part out and put them in the Air Fryer when it beeps.
5. Cook for another 5 minutes at 400º F. Put salt and pepper to taste.
6. Serve and enjoy!!!

Pepperoni and Cheese Pizza Chips

Preparation Time: 3 minutes
Cooking Time: 15 minutes
Total Time: 18 minutes
Servings: 2
Calories: 329 kcal

Ingredients:
- 4 Tsp. Olive Oil
- 1 Tbsp. Oregano
- Salt and Pepper
- 2 Large Potatoes
- 28g Diced Tomatoes
- 15g Pepperoni
- 40g Hard Cheese

Cooking Instructions:
1. Peel and chop your potatoes. Put oil in the Air Fryer and cook the potatoes at 360º F for 12 minutes.
2. Remove the Chips from the Air fryer to the Air Fryer Baking Pan.
3. Mix together diced tomatoes with the oregano and salt and pepper and put them over the chips in the baking pan.
4. Use more cheese and pepperoni to cover it.
5. Cook for another 3 minutes at 320º F.
6. Serve immediately!!!

Chewy Granola Bars

Preparation Time: 3 minutes
Cooking Time: 15 minutes
Total Time: 18 minutes
Servings: 6
Calories: 320 kcal

Ingredients:
- 1 Tsp. Vanilla Essence
- 250g Gluten Free Oats
- 60g Melted Butter
- 1 Tsp. Cinnamon
- Handful Raisins
- 30g Brown Sugar
- 3 Tbsp. Honey
- 1 Medium Peeled and Cooked Apple
- 1 Tbsp. Olive Oil

Cooking Instructions:
1. Blend the gluten free oats and put all other dry ingredients into the blender.
2. Put all the wet ingredients into Air Fryer baking pan and mix thoroughly with a small wooden spoon.
3. Pour the dry ingredients from the blender to the baking pan. Use fork to mix well.
4. Press down the mixture into the Air Fryer baking pan. Put the raisins and make it be at the same level.
5. Cook 360° F for 10 minutes. Turn-over and cook for another 5 minutes. Refrigerate for about 5 minutes.
6. Serve and enjoy!!!

Messy Sloppy Joes Cheesy Fries

Preparation Time: 15 minutes
Cooking Time: 30 minutes
Total Time: 45 minutes
Servings: 2

Ingredients:
- 1 Tbsp. Oregano
- 200g Minced Beef
- 200g Tin Tomatoes
- 2 Tbsp. Olive Oil
- 5 Medium Potatoes
- 1 Tsp. Basil
- 1 Tsp. Bolognese Seasoning
- Salt and Pepper
- 28g Cheddar Cheese
- 1 Tbsp. Garlic Puree
- 1 Tbsp. Tomato Puree
- 1 Tbsp. Thyme
- 1 Large Onion peeled and diced

Cooking Instructions:
1. Pre-heat your Air Fryer to 180º C for 5 minutes.
2. Peel and chop your potatoes and then put your chips in the Air Fryer and cook at 180º C for 20 minutes with a tbsp. of olive oil.
3. While it's still cooking, be shaking it at an interval of 7 minutes to make it not too dry.
4. With the remaining olive oil, cook the onions on a medium heat until they become soft.
5. Put the garlic puree, tomato puree, mince and cook for 10 minutes or until it becomes brownish.
6. Put all the seasoning and the tin tomatoes. You may reduce the heat.
7. Serve and enjoy!!!

Spam Fritters

Preparation Time: 5 minutes
Cooking Time: 8 minutes
Total Time: 13 minutes
Servings: 4
Calories: 639 kcal

Ingredients:
- 100g Plain Flour
- 400g Spam
- 28g Cheddar Cheese
- Salt and Pepper
- 200g Gluten Free Oats
- 1 Medium Egg Beaten

Cooking Instructions:
1. Get a popular blender and blend your gluten free oats.
2. Keep 3 small mixing bowls; put your plain flour in one bowl, beaten egg in another and gluten free oats in a third.
3. Stir in salt and pepper to the flour. Put grated cheddar cheese to your oats and stir.
4. Chop your spam into sticks and roll in the egg, roll in the flour and fully coat in the oats.
5. Cook as much as the number that will fit in your Air Fryer pan at once to avoid overcrowding for 8 minutes at 360º F.
6. Serve immediately and enjoy!!!

Sweet Potato Burger Buns

Preparation Time: 3 minutes
Cooking Time: 10 minutes
Total Time: 13 minutes
Servings: 4
Calories: 50 kcal

Ingredients:
- 1 Large Sweet Potato
- 4 Medium Paleo Burgers
- Salt and Pepper
- Hamburger Press
- 2 Tsp. Olive Oil

Cooking Instructions:
1. Peel and chop your sweet potatoes into the shapes of burger buns.
2. Get 2 medium slices for each burger you are making.
3. The Air Fryer may contain 13-15 slices at the same time to avoid being overcrowded.
4. Rub the olive oil over them with your hands and season with salt and pepper.
5. Cook in the Air Fryer at 360° F for 10 minutes.
6. Serve and enjoy!!!

VEGAN & VEGETARIAN

Sticky Pumpkin Wedges

Preparation Time: 5 minutes
Cooking Time: 25 minutes
Total Time: 30 minutes
Servings: 2

Ingredients:
- 1 Tsp. Turmeric
- ½ Medium Pumpkin
- 1 Lime juice only
- Salt and Pepper
- 1 Tbsp. Balsamic Vinegar
- 1 Tbsp. Paprika

Cooking Instructions:
1. Cut your pumpkin into medium sized wedges and put it into the Air Fryer pan.
2. Cook in Air Fryer at 180º C. for 20 minutes.
3. Open the Air Fryer and put half of your seasonings, vinegar and lime.
4. Flip them over to the other side using tongs.
5. Add the remaining ingredients and Air-fry again for another 5 minutes on the other side at 200º C.
6. Serve and enjoy!!!

Veggie Pakoras

Preparation time: 20 minutes
Cook time: 20 minutes
Total time: 40 minutes
Servings: 2

Ingredients:
- 3 ounces Indian Granola
- Leftover Vegetables
- 1 Large Sweet Potato, peeled and diced
- A pinch of salt
- Pepper to salt

Cooking Instructions:
1. Add the potatoes into the steamer basket and place in your Instant Pot.
2. Close and lock the lid in place. Select the Steam button to cook for 15 minutes. When the timer beeps, do a quick pressure release.
3. Add the cooked potatoes to the leftover vegetables and mash everything with a potato masher.
4. Blend the Indian granola in the blender until it resembles thick breadcrumbs. Add the salt and pepper.
5. Place the vegetables into pakora shapes. Roll the vegetables in the granola blend.
6. Add them on a baking sheet and place into the Air Fryer. Air fry for about 20 minutes at 180ºC.
7. Serve and enjoy!!!

Potato Wedges

Preparation Time: 2 minutes
Cooking Time: 25 minutes
Total Time: 27 minutes
Servings: 4
Calories: 159 kcal

Ingredients:
- 1 Tbsp. Olive Oil
- 4 Large Potatoes
- Salt and Pepper
- 1 Tbsp. Cajun Spice

Cooking Instructions:
1. Slice the potatoes into wedge shapes and put them in your Air Fryer.
2. Pour a tbsp. of olive oil and cook in your Air Fryer at 190º C for 25 minutes.
3. To have a nice and perfect cook, shake them about 3 times during cooking time.
4. When it is done, flip them into a plate, put salt and pepper and Cajun spice making sure all the potato wedges are coated equally.
5. Serve and enjoy!!!

Curly Fries

Preparation Time: 5 minutes
Cooking Time: 15 minutes
Total Time: 20 minutes
Servings: 4

Ingredients:
- 1 Tbsp. Homemade Tomato Ketchup
- 2 Large Potatoes
- Salt and Pepper
- 2 Tbsp. Olive Oil
- 2 Tbsp. Coconut Oil

Cooking Instructions:
1. Peel your potatoes and chop them into curly fries shape.
2. In a small mixing bowl, mix together the coconut oil, olive oil, and potatoes making sure they are all coated.
3. Put them in the Air Fryer and Air-fry at 180º C for 15 minutes.
4. Coat with salt and pepper garnish with homemade tomato ketchup.
5. Serve and enjoy!!!

Veggie Fritters

Preparation time: 15 minutes
Cook time: 15 minutes
Total time: 30 minutes
Servings: 2

Ingredients:
- 3 ounces of turmeric granola
- 1 large sweet potato, diced
- 100 g Courgette, diced
- 3 large carrots, peeled and diced
- 1 medium onion, diced
- 1 lime rind and juice
- Salt & pepper

Cooking Instructions:
1. Add the potato, courgette, carrots and onion into the bottom of your Instant Pot.
2. Select the Steam button to cook for 5 minutes. When the timer beeps, do a quick pressure release. Carefully open the lid and drain the vegetables.
3. Add the vegetables into a tea towel and squeeze out any excess moisture. Once they are drained place in a mixing bowl.
4. Blend the turmeric granola with a blender. Add them into a medium bowl with the drained vegetables.
5. Add salt and pepper along with the juice and rind of one lime. Give everything a good mix and form into fritter like shapes.
6. Refrigerate for at least an hour to harden. Add into your Air Fryer and cook for 15 minutes at 200º C.
7. Serve with my Paleo ranch dressing.

Vegetable Samosas

Preparation Time: 3 minutes
Cooking Time: 6 minutes
Total Time: 9 minutes
Servings: 12
Calories: 30 kcal

Ingredients:
- 200g Leftover Vegetable Korma
- 6 Weight Watchers Wraps
- Egg Wash

Cooking Instructions:
1. Chop up a wrap in half using a sterilized scissors, egg wash the inside of the wrap.
2. Create a kind of layer on one side of the half wrap with leftover vegetable samosa filling and hold down the other side.
3. Before putting in the Air Fryer, create a layer of egg wash. Rinse well and repeat putting about 4 in the Air Fryer at the same time.
4. Air-fry at 400º F for 3 minutes. Flip them over to the other side and Air-fry for another 3 minutes.
5. Continue until all the vegetable samosas are completely cooked.
6. Serve and enjoy!!!

Avocado on Toast

Preparation Time: 1 minute
Cooking Time: 8 minutes
Total Time: 9 minutes
Servings: 4
Calories: 109 kcal

Ingredients:
- 100g Mashed Avocado
- 4 Slices of Whole Wheat Bread

Cooking Instructions:
1. Add a slice of toast in the Air Fryer and Air-fry at 200º C for 4 minutes.
2. Flip them all over to the other side and Air-fry for another 4 minutes.
3. Use avocado and put on the top of it.
4. Serve and enjoy!!!

Grilled Tomatoes

Preparation Time: 1 minute
Cooking Time: 13 minutes
Total Time: 14 minutes
Servings: 3
Calories: 23 kcal

Ingredients:
- 1 Tsp. Oregano
- 3 Medium Beefcake Tomatoes
- Salt and Pepper

Cooking Instructions:
1. Cut the tomatoes into half to have equal sizes.
2. Put the tomatoes on top of the Air Fryer grill pan.
3. Add the oregano, pepper and salt. Cook at 360° F for 8 minutes.
4. Flip them over and Air-fry for another 5 minutes with same temperature.
5. Serve and enjoy!!!

Vegetable Fries

Preparation Time: 5 minutes
Cooking Time: 15 minutes
Total Time: 20 minutes
Servings: 4

Ingredients:
- 150g Sweet Potato
- 150g Courgette
- 150g Carrots
- 2 Tbsp. Olive Oil
- 1 Tsp. Thyme
- Pinch Mixed Spice
- Pinch Basil
- Salt and Pepper

Cooking Instructions:
1. Peel your sweet potatoes and carrots. Slice sweet potato, carrots and courgettes into chunky chips shape.
2. Add them in the Air Fryer with the olive oil and cook at 180º C for 18 minutes.
3. Flip them over to the other side two times at the interval of 5 minutes so they are cooked well.
4. Flip them onto serving plate, put the seasoning and shake properly.
5. Serve immediately and enjoy!!!

Pumpkin French Fries

Preparation Time: 5 minutes
Cooking Time: 15 minutes
Total Time: 20 minutes
Servings: 2

Cooking Ingredients:
- 1 Tbsp. Mustard
- 250g Pumpkin
- Salt and Pepper
- Whole 30 Tomato Ketchup optional
- 1 Tsp. Thyme

Cooking Instructions:
1. Wash and Peel the pumpkin, get the seeds out and chop into French Fries.
2. Put them in the Air Fryer and cook at 200º C for 15 minutes.
3. Flip over while it is still cooking and put mustard, thyme, pepper and salt. Garnish with tomato ketchup.
4. Serve and enjoy!!!

French Fries

Preparation Time: 5 minutes
Cooking Time: 30 minutes
Total Time: 35 minutes
Servings: 2
Calories: 317 kcal
Ingredients:
- 4 Tbsp. Olive Oil
- 4 Medium Potatoes
- Salt and Pepper

Cooking Instructions:
1. Peel your potatoes and chop them into smaller sizes.
2. Put them in your Air Fryer and put the olive oil.
3. Cook at 180º C and turn them at the following interval 2, 8 and 15 minutes respectively.
4. Air-fry for another 5 minutes at 200º C. Season with salt and pepper.
5. Serve and enjoy!!!

Crinkle Cut Chips

Preparation Time: 2 minutes
Cooking Time: 15 minutes
Total Time: 17 minutes
Servings: 4

Ingredients:
- 1 Large Potato
- Crinkle Cut Knife
- Salt and Pepper
- 1 Tbsp. Olive Oil

Cooking Instructions:
1. Peel your potato, chop them into crinkle cut chips using your crinkle cut knife.
2. Add salt and pepper. Put the chips in the olive oil.
3. Cook in the Air Fryer at 400° F for 15 minutes.
4. Halfway during cooking time, flip them over and continue cooking.
5. Top with homemade tomato ketchup.
6. Serve and enjoy!!!

Rosemary Roast Potatoes

Preparation Time: 2 minutes
Cooking Time: 10 minutes
Total Time: 12 minutes
Servings: 4
Calories: 93 kcal

Ingredients:
- 1 Tbsp. Olive Oil
- 2 Large Potatoes
- Salt and Pepper
- 1 Tsp. Rosemary

Cooking Instructions:
1. Peel your potatoes and chop them to be in the shape of roast potato.
2. Put a tbsp. of olive oil into your Air Fryer; put the chopped potatoes and Air-fry at 180º C for 10 minutes.
3. When they are well cooked, flip them onto a mixing bowl and pour salt, pepper and rosemary. Mix thoroughly.
4. Serve and enjoy!!!

Vegan Veggie Balls

Preparation time: 20 minutes
Cook time: 20 minutes
Total time: 40 minutes
Servings: 6
Calories: 142 kcal

Ingredients:

- 200 g cauliflower
- 100 g sweet potato
- 70 g carrot
- 90 g parsnips
- 2 teaspoons of garlic puree
- 1 teaspoon of chives
- 1 teaspoon of paprika
- 1 teaspoon of mixed spice
- 2 teaspoons of oregano
- ½ cup of desiccated coconut
- 1 cup of gluten free oats
- Salt & Pepper

Cooking Instructions:

1. Place all the vegetables in your food processor and whizz around until your raw vegetables looks like breadcrumbs.
2. Add them into a tea towel and squeeze out all the excess water to form a firm mixture.
3. Add them in a medium bowl and add the remaining ingredients. Give everything a good mix and form them into medium sized balls with your hands.
4. Refrigerate them for at least 2 hours to harden. Add them in the Air Fryer and cook for 160° C for 10 minutes.
5. Roll them over and cook for additional 10 minutes at 200° C.
6. Serve and enjoy!!!

Apple Chips

Preparation Time: 2 minutes
Cooking Time: 10 minutes
Total Time: 12 minutes
Servings: 4
Calories: 608 kcal

Ingredients:
- 1 Pinch Cinnamon
- 6 Large Red Apples
- 1 Tsp. Olive Oil

Cooking Instructions:
1. Chop your apple into small bite sizes.
2. Put a tbsp. of olive oil into your Air Fryer.
3. Add the chopped potatoes and Air-fry at 180º C for 10 minutes.
4. When they are well cooked, flip them onto a mixing bowl with cinnamon.
5. Serve immediately and enjoy!!!

Rosemary Sweet Potatoes

Preparation time: 2 minutes
Cook time: 20 minutes
Total time: 22 minutes
Servings: 2

Ingredients:
- 6 Sweet Potatoes
- 2 tablespoons of olive oil
- Handful Fresh Rosemary
- Salt & Pepper
- Paleo Ranch Dressing optional

Cooking Instructions:
1. Preheat your Air Fryer to 180°C.
2. Wash the rosemary in clean water and divide them into 2 piles.
3. Add one pile to one side and finely chop the other pile. Slice the sweet potato into bit slices.
4. Generously season the potatoes with salt and pepper and drizzle with olive oil.
5. Add them in your Air Fryer, sprinkle the small bits of rosemary over and air fry at 180°C for 15 minutes.
6. Shake them after 15 minutes and air fry for additional 5 minutes to crisp at 200°C. Season with fresh uncooked rosemary.
7. Serve immediately with some homemade Paleo ranch dressing.

Spicy Sweet Potato Wedges

Preparation time: 5 minutes
Cook time: 20 minutes
Total time: 25 minutes
Servings: 2

Ingredients:
- 2 large sweet potatoes, peeled and chopped into shape of wedges
- 1 tablespoon of Mexican seasoning
- 1 teaspoon of cumin
- 1 teaspoon of mustard powder
- 1 teaspoon of chili powder
- 1 tablespoon of olive oil
- Pinch of salt
- Pinch of pepper

Cooking Instructions:
1. Preheat your Air Fryer for 5 minutes at 180ºC.
2. In a medium bowl, add all the seasonings and give everything a good mix.
3. Add the potato wedges, and toss everything to cover.
4. Add the potato wedges in your Air Fryer, sprinkle with olive oil.
5. Cook for about 20 minutes. Shake the Air Fryer basket every 5 minutes until they are cooked.
6. Sprinkle with a little extra chili powder and serve immediately.

BURGER RECIPES

Lamb Burgers

Preparation Time: 3 minutes
Cooking Time: 18 minutes
Total Time: 21 minutes
Servings: 4
Calories: 478 kcal
Ingredients:
Lamb Burgers:
- 1 Tbsp. Moroccan Spice
- Salt and Pepper
- 2 Tsp. Garlic Puree
- 1 Tsp. Harissa Paste
- 650g Minced Lamb

Greek Dip:
- ½ Tsp. Oregano
- 1 Small Lemon juice
- 3 Tbsp. Greek Yoghurt
- 1 Tsp. Moroccan Spice

Cooking Instructions:
1. Put your lamb burger ingredients in a mixing bowl and mix thoroughly.
2. Make the minced mixture into lamb burger shapes using a burger press.
3. Put the lamb burgers in the Air Fryer and Air-fry at 360º F for 18 minutes.
4. Make your Greek Dip while the lamb burgers are still cooking.
5. Use a fork to mix the Greek dip ingredients together and top with your lamb burgers.
6. Serve and enjoy!!!

Chicken Avocado Burgers

Preparation Time: 2 minutes
Cooking Time: 12 minutes
Total Time: 14 minutes
Servings: 2
Calories: 707 kcal
Ingredients:
- 400g Avocado
- 400g Minced Chicken
- 1 Tbsp. Mexican Seasoning

Cooking Instructions:

1. Peel and cut your avocado. Use only 3 and cut into small cubes.
2. In a small mixing bowl, put your minced chicken together with your chunks of avocado and Mexican seasoning. Mix them thoroughly.
3. Create them into shapes of chicken burger patty.
4. Air-fry at 360° F for 12 minutes.
5. Serve and enjoy!!!

Lentil Burgers

Preparation Time: 10 minutes
Cooking Time: 30 minutes
Total Time: 40 minutes
Servings: 4

Ingredients:
- 1 Tbsp. Garlic Puree
- Handful Fresh Basil cleaned and chopped
- Salt and Pepper
- 1 Large Carrot peeled and grated
- 1 Large Onion peeled and diced
- 100g White Cabbage
- 300g Gluten Free Oats
- 4 Vegan Burger Buns
- 100g Black Beluga Lentils
- 1 Tsp. Cumin

Cooking Instructions:
1. Put your gluten free oats in the blender and blend until it looks like flour.
2. Put the lentils in a saucepan and cover with enough water. Cook on a medium heat for 45 minutes.
3. Using the steam function, steam the vegetables in your Instant Pot for 5 minutes.
4. Drain the lentils, put them in a bowl with the steamed vegetables with the oats and put the seasoning. Form them into burgers.
5. Put the burgers in the Air Fryer and cook at 180º C for 30 minutes. Garnish with salad.
6. Serve and enjoy

Juicy Lucy Cheese Burger

Preparation time: 5 minutes
Cook time: 15 minutes
Total time: 20 minutes
Servings: 2
Calories: 553 kcal

Ingredients:
- 250 g minced beef
- 1 large onion, diced
- 100 g cheddar cheese
- 1 teaspoon of mixed herbs

- Salt & Pepper

Cooking Instructions:
1. Preheat the Air Fryer to 180ºC. In a medium bowl, add the diced onion, minced beef and seasoning.
2. Give everything a good mix and roll them into 4 even sized balls. Add them on the chopping board and squash the burgers down into bit pieces.
3. Add half of the cheese in between two of the burgers and merge them together to form a burger, then the cheese and then the 2nd burger.
4. Repeat the same procedure for burger 3 and 4 too. Ensure that you pinch around the sides to hide the cheese.
5. Add the 2 burgers in your Air Fryer and cook for 15 minutes at 180º C. Remove the burgers out and use a knife or cake tester to check whether the cheese has melted in the center.
6. Once the juices run clear, then your burgers are cooked. Add them in the Air Fryer if they don't run clear and cook for additional 10 minutes.
7. Serve in a burger bun with loads of garnish.

Falafel Burger

Preparation Time: 3 minutes
Cooking Time: 15 minutes
Total Time: 18 minutes
Servings: 2
Calories: 709 kcal

Ingredients:
- 1 Small Lemon
- 140g Gluten Free Oats
- 400g Can Chickpeas
- 1 Tbsp. Coriander
- 1 Tbsp. Oregano
- 1 Small Red Onion
- 28g Cheese
- 4 Tbsp. Soft Cheese
- 1 Tbsp. Garlic Puree
- 1 Tbsp. Parsley
- Salt and Pepper
- 28g Feta Cheese
- 3 Tbsp. Greek Yoghurt

Cooking Instructions:
1. Put all the seasonings (garlic, the lemon rind, red onion and the drained chickpeas) into a blender, the.
2. Blend until they are coarse. In a mixing bowl, mix together ½ of the soft cheese, hard cheese and the feta.
3. Prepare them to have burger shapes. Roll them in gluten free oats until chickpea mixture are invisible.
4. Put them in the Air Fryer baking pan and cook at 360º F for 8 minutes.
5. In a mixing bowl, put the rest of the soft cheese, Greek Yoghurt, salt and pepper.
6. Give everything a good mix. Add the juice of the lemon and mix all together.
7. Serve and enjoy!!!

Veggie Burgers

Preparation time: 6 minutes
Cook time: 25 minutes
Total time: 31 minutes
Servings: 6
Calories: 373 kcal

Ingredients:
- 500 g sweet potato, peeled and chopped
- 800 g cauliflower, chopped
- 190 g carrots, chopped
- 1 cup of chickpeas
- 2 cups of whole meal breadcrumbs
- 1 cup of grated mozzarella cheese
- 1 tablespoon of mixed herbs
- 1 tablespoon of basil
- Salt & Pepper

Cooking Instructions:
1. Add the chopped vegetables into the inner liner of your Instant Pot and pour 1 cup of water.
2. Close and lock the lid in place and ensure that the valve is in sealing position. Select Manual, High Pressure for 10 minutes.
3. When the timer beeps, do a quick pressure release. Carefully open the lid and remove the vegetables. Use a tea towel to squeeze out the excess moisture.
4. Add the chickpeas and mash the vegetables together. Add the breadcrumbs and give everything a good mix.
5. Add the seasonings and use your hands to make them into veggie burger shapes. Roll in the grated cheese to be completely covered in cheese.
6. Add the shaped veggie burgers in your Air Fryer cook 180° C/360° F for about 10 minutes. Cook for additional 5 minutes at 200° C/400° F to make them crusty.
7. Serve warm in bread buns or with a salad and enjoy.

Bunless Burgers

Preparation Time: 5 minutes
Cooking Time: 20 minutes
Total Time: 25 minutes
Servings: 4

Ingredients:
- 1 Medium Avocado
- Handful Green Beans
- Handful Lettuce
- 3 Medium Tomatoes
- 400g Minced Beef
- 1 Small Red Onion
- 4 Slices Back Bacon
- 1 Tbsp. Parsley
- Salt and Pepper
- 1 Tbsp. Tomato Puree
- 1 Tbsp. Olive Oil
- Handful Fresh Thyme
- Handful Fresh Basil

Cooking Instructions:
1. Preheat the Air Fryer to 180º C.
2. Clean and mince your fresh herbs. Peel and dice the avocado, red onion and fresh tomato.
3. In a mixing bowl, put the minced beef, $1/5$ of the red onion, all the seasonings, tomato puree and mix properly. Prepare them to have 4 burger shapes.
4. Put the baking mat at the bottom of the Air Fryer. Put the burgers onto the baking pan and cook in the Air Fryer at 360º F for 10 minutes.
5. Put the green beans in olive oil and put in the Air Fryer with the burgers and cook for 5 minutes.
6. Add the slices of bacon and cook for another 5 minutes. Garnish with salad.
7. Serve and enjoy!!!

Spicy Courgette and Chickpea Burgers

Preparation Time: 5 minutes
Cooking Time: 10 minutes
Total Time: 15 minutes
Servings: 4
Calories: 119 kcal

Ingredients:
- 30g Cheddar Cheese

- 1 Tsp. Garlic Puree
- 1 Can Chickpeas drained
- 1 Large Courgette, spiralized and well drained
- Fresh Chives
- Salt and Pepper
- 2 Medium Eggs beaten
- 3 Tbsp. Coriander
- 1 Tsp. Chili Powder
- 1 Tsp. Mixed Spice
- 30g Plain Flour
- 1 Tsp. Cumin
- 1 Red Onion peeled and finely diced

Cooking Instructions:
1. Put the drained chickpeas and onion and mash well in a large mixing bowl.
2. Add the flour, the spiralized courgette, seasoning and cheese. Mix thoroughly!!!
3. Add the eggs and mix them into burger shapes. Pour more flour if you realized it is too sloppy.
4. Air-fryer at 180º C for 15 minutes. Top with fresh chives.
5. Serve and enjoy!!!

Chicken Burgers

Preparation Time: 3 minutes
Cooking Time: 18 minutes
Total Time: 21 minutes
Servings: 4
Calories: 346 kcal

Cooking Ingredients:
- 1 Tbsp. Oregano
- 450g Minced Chicken
- Salt and Pepper
- 100g Whole-meal Breadcrumbs
- 50g Mozzarella Cheese

Cooking Instructions:
1. In a small mixing bowl and add the minced chicken.
2. Season with salt and pepper and oregano and add ¾ of the breadcrumbs. Mix properly to coat the seasoning well.
3. Create a kind of burger shapes, roll each burger in the cheese and then in the leftover breadcrumbs making sure that all the sides are coated properly.
4. Put in the Air Fryer and cook at 360º F for 18 minutes.
5. Serve and enjoy!!!

Cauliflower Veggie Burger

Preparation time: 25 minutes
Cook time: 20 minutes
Total time: 45 minutes
Servings: 8
Calories: 219 kcal

Ingredients:
- 1 Kilo Cauliflower, chopped into florets
- 3 Teaspoon of Coconut Oil
- 2 Teaspoons of Garlic Puree
- 1 Cup of Bread Crumbs
- ¼ Desiccated Coconut
- ½ Cup of Oats
- 3 Tablespoons of Plain Flour
- 1 Large Egg, beaten
- 2 Cups of Herby Bread Crumbs
- 1 Teaspoon of Mustard Powder
- 2 Teaspoons of Thyme
- 2 Teaspoons of Parsley
- 2 Teaspoons of Chives
- 1 Teaspoon of Mixed Spice
- Salt & Pepper

Cooking Instructions:
1. Steam the cauliflower florets in the soup maker for 25 minutes. Remove the cauliflower and leave in the soup maker.
2. Dice the cauliflower into bite small pieces with a vegetable knife. Add salt, pepper, mustard and a teaspoon of garlic puree.
3. Place in a blender and blend for a few minutes and then drain over the sink. Add the cauliflower into a tea towel and drain out any excess water until it looks like bread dough.
4. Add the cauliflower in a medium bowl with salt and pepper, remaining seasoning, further garlic puree, coconut oil and give everything a good mix.
5. Add the desiccated coconut, oats and one cup of bread crumbs and give everything a good mix. Cover your hands in flour to avoid sticking to the burgers.
6. Use your hands to shape them into burgers. Roll in the flour, the egg and the herby bread crumbs. Add in your Air Fryer and cook for 10 minutes on each side at 180º C.
7. Serve immediately with my healthy ranch dressing and with salad garnish and a burger bun.

King Whopper Burger

Preparation Time: 8 minutes
Cooking Time: 10 minutes
Total Time: 18 minutes
Servings: 4
Calories: 491 kcal
Ingredients:
- Avocado Sauce
- 1 Small Avocado
- 400g Lean Minced Pork
- 4 Whole-meal Burger Buns
- 1 Small Onion peeled and diced
- 1 Tbsp. Worcester Sauce
- 1 Tbsp. Tomato Ketchup
- 1 Tsp. Parsley
- Salt and Pepper
- 1 Tsp. Garlic Puree
- 1 Tsp. Mixed Herbs
- 2 Tbsp. Spring Onion
- 1 Tsp. Thyme
- Salad Garnish sliced tomato, lettuce, cucumber

Cooking Instructions:
1. In a mixing bowl, mix together your diced onion, ½ of your Avocado, ½ your spring onion and all the seasoning.
2. Prepare them in the form of burgers and put them in the refrigerator.
3. Preheat your Air Fryer at 180º C for 10 minutes.
4. Put your burgers in the Air Fryer and cook at 360º F for 12 minutes.
5. Layer the bottom of a burger bun with salad garnish when the burgers are done.
6. Add the burger, sliced avocado and avocado sauce.
7. Serve and enjoy!!!

Hamburgers

Preparation Time: 3 minutes
Cooking Time: 17 minutes
Total Time: 20 minutes
Servings: 2
Calories: 774 kcal
Ingredients:
- 2 Medium Potatoes
- 2 Slices Mozzarella Cheese

- 2 Whole Wheat Dinner Rolls
- 1 Tsp. Mustard
- Salt and Pepper
- 320g Mixed Mince
- ¼ Small Onion
- ½ Tsp. Olive Oil
- 2 Tsp. Mixed Herbs

Cooking Instructions:
1. Peel and cut the potatoes into French Fries.
2. Add them in ½ tsp. of olive oil and set aside. Peel and mince your onion.
3. In a small mixing bowl, put the mixed mince and the seasonings. Prepare the mixture to have hamburger patty shapes.
4. Add them into Air Fryer and set aside. Cook in the Air Fryer at 360° F for 15 minutes.
5. Add a slice of mozzarella cheese on top of both burgers and then cook for another 2 minutes at 320° F.
6. Serve immediately and enjoy!!!

KFC Zinger Chicken Burger

Preparation Time: 10 minutes
Cooking Time: 15 minutes
Total Time: 25 minutes
Servings: 4
Calories: 549 kcal

Ingredients:
- 10ml KFC Spice Blend
- 50g Plain Flour
- 1 Tsp. Paprika
- Salt and Pepper
- 100ml Bread Crumbs
- 1 Tsp. Worcester Sauce
- 1 Tsp. Mustard Powder
- 6 Chicken Breasts
- 1 Small Egg beaten

Cooking Instructions:
1. In a food processor, mince your chicken with mustard, Worcester sauce, paprika, pepper and salt.
2. Prepare your chicken in burger shapes and set aside. Get 3 mixing bowls. Put your egg in one bowl.
3. Add your flour, put your KFC spice blend in the third bowl and mix with your bread crumbs.
4. Cover your Zinger burgers in the flour, the egg and then the bread crumbs.
5. Put in the Air Fryer at 180º C for 15 minutes.
6. Serve and enjoy!!!

Nandos Beanie Burger

Preparation Time: 5 minutes
Cooking Time: 12 minutes
Total Time: 17 minutes
Servings: 4

Ingredients:
- 1 Tbsp. Homemade Nandos Marinade
- 2 Cans Black Beans
- ½ Onion
- 1 Red Onion
- 8 Medium Slices Whole-meal Bread
- 3 Garlic Cloves
- 1 Lime juice and rind
- 1 Tbsp. Paprika
- 1 Tbsp. Cumin
- Salt and Pepper
- 6 Bread Buns
- Salad Garnish

Cooking Instructions:
1. Wash the black beans; sieve properly in order to remove excess water.
2. Blend the sliced bread into breadcrumbs. Peel and mince the garlic and onions.
3. Put the breadcrumbs in a mixing bowl including all the seasoning, black beans, garlic and onions.
4. In the marinade, put the lime and mix properly.
5. Create 6 medium shaped burgers. Put in a refrigerator for an hour.
6. Air-fry at 347º F for 12 minutes. Garnish with salad and homemade ketchup.
7. Serve and enjoy!!!

Mediterranean Paleo Burgers

Preparation Time: 3 minutes
Cooking Time: 15 minutes
Total Time: 18 minutes
Servings: 2
Calories: 585 kcal

Ingredients:
- 1 Tsp. Garlic Puree
- 2 Tsp. Oregano
- 350g Mixed Mince

- Sweet Potato Fries
- ¼ Small Onion
- ½ Tsp. Rosemary
- Salt and Pepper
- 2 Tbsp. Fried Onions
- 1 Tsp. Thyme
- 1 Tsp. Parsley
- 2 Fried Eggs

Cooking Instructions:
1. Peel and mince the ¼ of an onion.
2. In a small mixing bowl, put the mixed mince, garlic and onion.
3. Mix thoroughly and make into hamburger shapes.
4. Put in the Air Fryer at 360º F for 15 minutes. Garnish with fried onions or egg.
5. Serve and enjoy!!!

Double Cheese Burger

Preparation Time: 5 minutes
Cook Time: 22 minutes
Total Time: 27 minutes
Servings: 4
Calories: 577 kcal

Ingredients:
- 4 Burger Buns
- 500 g Pork, minced
- 1 Large Onion, diced
- ½ Small Onion, peeled and sliced
- 100 g Cheddar Cheese
- 1 Tablespoon of Soft Cheese
- Salt & Pepper

Cooking Instructions:
1. In a medium bowl, add the minced pork, diced onion, seasoning and the soft cheese.
2. Give everything a good mix to form a big ball of meat. Divide them into 8 even sized burgers. Add 4 of your burgers into your Air Fryer.
3. Cook at 180º C for about 10 minutes. Remove them and add them on a baking tray and sprinkle with cheese on top.
4. While the other burgers are still cooking in your Air Fryer, take the cooked burgers from the baking tray and add them in your oven on low for 10 minutes.
5. Once the burgers are 5 minutes away from being done, add the sliced onion in saucepan with a drizzle of olive oil and sauté for a couple of minutes.
6. Once the burgers are done, garnish with salad at the bottom of the bun with a burger on top.
7. Press the other burger on top and sprinkle with more cheese along with some fried onion.
8. Serve immediately and enjoy!!!

SNACKS & APPETIZERS

Flaky Buttermilk Biscuits

Preparation Time: 5 minutes
Cooking Time: 8 minutes
Total Time: 13 minutes
Servings: 16
Calories: 192 kcal

Ingredients:
- 500ml Buttermilk
- 530g Self Raising Flour
- 120g Butter

Cooking Instructions:
1. In a small mixing bowl, put flour and butter and rub fat into the flour. Repeat it for several times. Pour the buttermilk into the bowl and mix properly with a fork.
2. Dip your hands into the flour and use your hands to prepare the mixture into a dough ball.
3. Use a biscuit cutter to make about 16 medium sized flaky biscuits.
4. Put in the Air Fryer grill pan at the rate of 4 biscuits at a time. Avoid overcrowding and do not allow them to touch each other.
5. Cook each set of 4 in the Air Fryer at $360°$ F for 8 minutes.
6. Serve immediately and enjoy!!!

Balsamic Glazed Chicken

Preparation Time: 3 hours 5 minutes
Cooking Time: 12 minutes
Total Time: 3 hours 17 minutes
Servings: 2
Ingredients:
- 15 Tsp. Olive Oil
- 1 Tbsp. Parsley
- 2 Chicken Breasts
- 1 Large Mango
- 1 Tbsp. Oregano
- 1 Medium Avocado
- 1 Red Pepper
- 5 Tbsp. Balsamic Vinegar
- Pinch Mustard Powder
- Salt and Pepper
- Fresh Parsley to garnish
- 4 Garlic Cloves

Cooking Instructions:
1. Start by Peeling and removing the stone from your mango. Dice ¼ of the mango and set aside ¾ of it.
2. Add all the seasonings into a blender along with the diced mango, olive oil, garlic and the balsamic vinegar and blend.
3. Put the liquid into a bowl, put whole chicken breasts and put it in a refrigerator for 3 hours. Take away the chicken from the marinade.
4. Add them inside the Air Fryer grill pan. Add a layer of the marinade onto the top of the chicken using a pastry brush.
5. Cook in the Air Fryer at 180º C for 12 minutes. After 6 minutes, flip the chicken to the other side.
6. While it is still cooking, slice the avocado, pepper and mango and top with fresh parsley.
7. Serve and enjoy!!!

Sweet Potato Fries

Preparation Time: 5 minutes
Cooking Time: 15 minutes
Total Time: 20 minutes
Servings: 2
Calories: 319 kcal
Ingredients:
- 1 Tsp. Mustard Powder

- 300g Sweet Potatoes
- Salt and Pepper
- 3 Tbsp. Olive Oil

Cooking Instructions:
1. Peel and chop up your sweet potatoes into some chunky chips.
2. Put 2 tbsp. of olive oil into the Air Fryer, put the sweet potatoes and turn them.
3. Cook in the Air Fryer at 180º C for 15 minutes. After 6 minutes, flip the sweet potatoes to the other side so that they are well cooked.
4. Remove from the Air Fryer into a bowl when they are well cooked.
5. Put the remaining tbsp. of olive oil along with the seasoning and mix thoroughly.
6. Serve and enjoy!!!

Crinkle Cut Chips

Preparation Time: 2 minutes
Cooking Time: 15 minutes
Total Time: 17 minutes
Servings: 4

Ingredients:
- 1 Tbsp. Olive Oil
- 1 Large Potato
- Salt and Pepper

Cooking Instructions:
1. Peel your potato.
2. Chop them into crinkle cut chips on your chopping board with your crinkle cut knife.
3. Put salt and pepper to the crinkle cut chips. Put the crinkle cut chips in the olive oil.
4. Cook in the Air Fryer at 200º C for 15 minutes.
5. After 7 minutes, flip the potatoes to the other side so that they are well cooked.
6. Top with homemade tomato ketchup.
7. Serve and enjoy!!!

Roasted Parsnips

Preparation Time: 2 minutes
Cooking Time: 11 minutes
Total Time: 13 minutes
Servings: 4
Calories: 174 kcal

Ingredients:
- 6 Medium Parsnips
- Salt and Pepper

Cooking Instructions:
1. Peel your parsnips and then chop to have a shape like roasted parsnip.
2. Put them into your Instant Pot steamer basket. Lower the basket into your Instant Pot and put it on top of the trivet.
3. Put a cup of warm water into the parsnips and lock the lid on your Instant Pot.
4. Make sure the valve is set to sealing position and cook for 3 minutes on manual pressure. When the timer beeps, quickly release pressure.
5. Drain the parsnips, put them on a chopping board and season with salt and pepper. Cook the parsnip in the Air Fryer at 200º C for 11 minutes.
6. After 5 minutes, flip them over to the other side so that they are well cooked.
7. Serve immediately and enjoy!!!

Cheese Toastie

Preparation Time: 1 minutes
Cooking Time: 8 minutes
Total Time: 9 minutes
Servings: 4
Calories: 302 kcal
Ingredients:
- 8 Slices Whole-meal Bread
- 150g Cheddar Cheese

Cooking Instructions:
1. Stock up your cheese and bread into yummy cheese sandwiches.
2. Put 2 at a time into the Air Fryer and cook at 180º C for 4 minutes on each sides.
3. Serve immediately and enjoy!!!

Buttermilk Fried Chicken

Preparation Time: 5 minutes
Cooking Time: 16 minutes
Total Time: 21 minutes
Servings: 4
Ingredients:
Buttermilk Marinade:
- 2 Cups of buttermilk
- 1 Tsp. paprika
- 2 Tsp. salt
- 2 Tsp. black pepper

Flour Mixture:
- 2 Cups of flour
- 1 Tbsp. of garlic powder
- 4 Boneless Chicken Breasts
- 1 Tbsp. of baking powder

Cooking Instructions:
1. Prepare your buttermilk and flour mixture.

2. Mix properly and then put the chicken. Preheat your Air Fryer at 360º F.
3. Dip your chicken into the buttermilk mixture, and then put it in the flour mixture.
4. Put them in the air fryer basket and cook at 360º F for 8 minutes.
5. Flip the chicken over and cook for another 8 minutes.
6. Serve and enjoy!!!

Flourless Chicken Cordon Bleu

Preparation Time: 5 minutes
Cooking Time: 30 minutes
Total Time: 35 minutes
Servings: 2

Ingredients:
- 1 Tbsp. Soft Cheese
- 2 Chicken Breasts
- 1 Small Egg beaten
- 1 Tsp. Garlic Puree
- 1 Slice Cheddar Cheese
- 1 Slice Ham
- 20g Oats
- 1 Tbsp. Thyme
- Salt and Pepper
- 1 Tsp. Parsley
- 1 Tbsp. Tarragon

Cooking Instructions:
1. Preheat your Air Fryer to 180º C. Put your chicken breast on a chopping board.
2. Chop them diagonally to enable you to fold them and put ingredients at the center. Put salt, pepper and tarragon to all sides of your chicken.
3. In a mixing bowl, put the soft cheese, garlic and parsley and mix properly. Place a layer of the cheese mixture in the middle along with ½ a slice each of the cheddar cheese and the ham.
4. Hold down on the chicken to be as if it is sealed with a layer of filling inside it. Get 2 mixing bowl. Put egg in one bowl; put the blended oats in another bowl.
5. In the blended oats bowl, put the thyme and mix properly. Roll the chicken in the first bowl, put it in the second bowl and then back to the first bowl.
6. Put your chicken pieces on a baking pan in your Air Fryer and cook at 180º C for 30 minutes. After 20 minutes flip them over so that both sides will be well cooked.
7. Serve and enjoy!!!

Airy Breaded Chicken Bread

Preparation Time: 8 minutes
Cooking Time: 18 minutes
Total Time: 26 minutes
Servings: 2

Ingredients:
- 1 Tsp. of Italian seasoning
- 5 Tbsp. of vegetable oil

- 2 Eggs, cracked and mixed in a bowl
- 1 Cup of breadcrumbs or panko
- 2 Pieces of chicken breast

Cooking Instructions:
1. Preheat your Air Fryer to 350º F.
2. Get 2 mixing bowl. Break your eggs and mix them in one bowl.
3. In another bowl, mix together the breadcrumbs or panko, Italian seasoning, and oil.
4. Burry the chicken into the egg and breadcrumb mixture.
5. Put them in your Air Fryer basket. Put enough oil to cover the chicken.
6. Cook the chicken in the Air Fryer at 180º C for 18 minutes.
7. After 10 minutes, flip them over to the other side and spray more oil so that they are well cooked.
8. Serve and enjoy!!!

Steak & French Fries

Preparation Time: 5 minutes
Cooking Time: 16 minutes
Total Time: 21 minutes
Servings: 2
Calories: 634 kcal

Ingredients:
- 1 Tsp. Bacon Olive Oil
- 2 Tsp. Garlic Butter
- 2 Rump Steaks
- 500g White Potatoes
- Salt and Pepper

Cooking Instructions:
1. Peel and slice your potatoes into French Fries.
2. In a mixing bowl, put the potatoes and season them with salt and pepper.
3. Put the bacon olive oil and mix with your hands so that the potatoes will be well coated.
4. Put the potatoes in the Air Fryer and cook at 350º F for 10 minutes.
5. Pound the rump steaks with a tenderizer and season with salt and pepper.
6. When the air fryer beeps, shake the potatoes and be sure no potatoes are stuck to the Air Fryer basket.
7. Put the pounded steaks on top of the fries and cook at 350º F for another 6 minutes.
8. Put a small portion of garlic butter over each steak before serving.
9. Serve and enjoy!!!

Cheese and Bacon Chips

Preparation Time: 3 minutes
Cooking Time: 17 minutes
Total Time: 20 minutes
Servings: 2

Ingredients:
- 2 Tsp. Olive Oil
- 2 Medium Potatoes
- 20g Cheddar Cheese grated
- Salt and Pepper
- 4 Bacon Rashers

Cooking Instructions:
1. Preheat your Air Fryer to 180º C.
2. Peel and chop your potatoes. Put them in the Air Fryer with a tsp. of olive oil over them.
3. Cook at 180º C for 10 minutes. Cut out the fat from your bacon and cut into bacon bits.
4. When the Air Fryer has finished, flip them over and put the bacon. Cook for another 5 minutes.
5. Flip again, put a tsp. olive oil and cook at 200º C for another 2 minutes. Put salt, pepper and grated cheese.
6. Serve and enjoy!!!

Crispy Southern Fried Chicken

Preparation Time: 5 minutes
Cooking Time: 25 minutes
Total Time: 30 minutes
Servings: 4
Ingredients:
- 50g Cauliflower
- 1 Large Egg beaten
- 2 Tbsp. Mustard Powder
- 8 Chicken Drumsticks
- 50g Gluten Free Oats
- 2 Tbsp. Oregano
- 1 Tsp. Cayenne Pepper
- Salt and Pepper
- 50ml Coconut Milk
- 2 Tbsp. Thyme

Cooking Instructions:
1. Preheat your Air Fryer to 180ºC.
2. Sprinkle salt and pepper on your chicken on a chopping board and then rub coconut milk on the chicken.
3. Exception of the egg, put everything into the blender little by little. Blend until it resembles breadcrumbs.
4. In 2 different mixing bowls, put the mixture in one bowl while you put the egg in another bowl.
5. Dip each chicken into the mixture, dip into the egg and then dip into the breadcrumbs finally.
6. Put 4 chicken pieces into your Air Fryer baking pan to avoid overcrowding and cook at 180º C for 20 minutes.
7. Flip them over and cook for another 5 minutes at 200º C so that it can be well cooked.
8. Serve and enjoy!!!

DESSERT RECIPES

Cinnamon Rolls

Preparation Time: 10 minute
Cooking Time: 9 minutes
Total Time: 19 minutes
Servings: 8
Ingredients:

- 1 Lb. frozen bread dough, thawed
- ¼ cup of butter, melted and cooled
- ¾ cup of brown sugar
- 1 Lb. frozen bread dough, thawed
- 1½ tbsp. ground cinnamon
- 1 Lb. frozen bread dough, thawed

Cream Cheese Glaze:
- ½ tsp. vanilla
- 4 Oz. cream cheese, softened
- 1¼ cups of powdered sugar

Cooking Instructions:
1. Spread flour on a flat surface and roll the dough into a rectangular size of 13 inch by 11 inch.
2. Brush the melted butter all over the dough, leaving a 1-inch border uncovered along the edge farthest away from you.
3. In a small mixing bowl, mix the brown sugar and cinnamon. Pour the mixture on the buttered dough. Do not cover the 1-inch border.
4. Start with the edge closest to you and roll the dough into a log and be sure to roll evenly and push out any air pockets.
5. Press the dough onto the roll when you get to the uncovered edge of the dough in order to seal it together.
6. Chop the log into 8 pieces and slowly slice them but do not over flatten the dough. Turn the slices to their sides, cover with a clean kitchen towel.
7. Allow the rolls sit in for about 1½ to 2 hours so that it can rise well. For the glaze, put the cream cheese and butter in a microwave-safe bowl.
8. Put it in the microwave to soften it for about 30 seconds at a time until it is easy to stir. Put the powdered sugar and stir to mix properly.
9. Put the vanilla extract and whisk until smooth. At this point, your rolls must have risen. Pre-heat your Air Fryer to 350º F.
10. Put the rolls into the Air Fryer basket, 4 at a time. Cook 180º C for 5 minutes. Flip the rolls over and cook for another 4 minutes.
11. Repeat with the remaining 4 rolls with the same temperature. For glazing, it does not need the rolls to be hot.
12. Allow it to cool for some minutes before glazing. Apply enough cream cheese glaze on top of the warm cinnamon rolls.
13. Serve and enjoy!!!

Apple Fries with Caramel Cream Dip

Preparation Time: 5 minutes
Cooking Time: 7 minutes
Total Time: 12 minutes
Servings: 8

Ingredients:
- 3 Eggs, beaten
- 1 Cup of graham cracker crumbs
- 3 Pink Lady or Honey crisp apples, peeled, cored and cut into 8 wedges
- ½ Cup of flour
- ¼ Cup of sugar
- ½ Cup of caramel sauce for garnish
- 8 Oz. whipped cream cheese

Cooking Instructions:
1. In a large mixing bowl, mix together the apple slices and flour.
2. Get 2 small mixing bowls. Put the beaten eggs in one bowl and mix the crushed graham crackers and sugar in the second bowl.
3. Dip each apple slice into the graham cracker crumbs, and then into the egg. Coat the slices on all sides and place the coated slices on a cookie sheet.
4. Pre-heat the Air Fryer to 380° F. Put oil into the Air Fryer basket. Cook the apples in batches. Put one layer of apple slices in the Air Fryer basket with oil.
5. Cook at 180° C for 5 minutes. Flip them over and cook for another 2 minutes. While apples are cooking prepare caramel cream dip.
6. Mix the whipped cream cheese and caramel sauce together. Turn the Caramel Cream Dip into a serving bowl.
7. Serve immediately and enjoy!!!

Sugared Dough Dippers with Chocolate Amaretto Sauce

Preparation Time: 5 minutes
Cooking Time: 8 minutes
Total Time: 13 minutes
Servings: 12

Ingredients:
- ½ Cup of butter, melted
- 1 Cup of sugar
- 2 Tbsp. Amaretto liqueur
- 1 Cup of heavy cream
- 1 Lb. bread dough, defrosted
- 12 Oz. good quality semi-sweet chocolate chips

Cooking Instructions:
1. Roll the dough into 2 (15-inch) logs. Cut each log into 20 slices. Cut each slice in half and twist the dough halves together about 4 times.
2. Put the dough on a cookie sheet and Spray the dough with melted butter and sprinkle sugar. Pre-heat the air fryer to 350º F.
3. Put melted butter into the Air Fryer basket. The dough twists are to be cooked in batches. Put about 10 to 12 dough twists in the Air Fryer basket.
4. Cook at 180º C for 5 minutes. Flip the dough strips over to the other side and brush with butter. Cook for another 3 minutes.
5. Make the chocolate amaretto sauce while dough is cooking. Bring the heavy cream to a simmer over medium heat.
6. In a large mixing bowl, put the chocolate chips and pour the hot cream over the chocolate chips. Stir until the chocolate starts to melt.
7. Change to a wire whisk and whisk until the chocolate is completely melted and the sauce. Stir in the Amaretto and flip onto a serving plate.
8. When the dough twists are done, put them in a small plate, brush with melted butter and coat with sugar.
9. Serve and enjoy!!!

Mini Cherry and Cheese Streusel Tartlets

Preparation Time: 10 minutes
Cooking Time: 19 minutes
Total Time: 29 minutes
Servings: 6

Ingredients:
- 1 Egg
- 6 Oz. cream cheese, softened
- 3 Tbsp. sugar

- 6 Packaged mini graham cracker tartlet crusts
- 1 Tbsp. all-purpose flour
- 2 Cups of cherry pie filling
- ½ Tsp. vanilla extract

Streusel Topping:
- 5 Tbsp. all-purpose flour
- ⅓ Cup of walnuts, chopped
- 3 Tbsp. melted butter
- 2 Tbsp. sugar
- ½ Tsp. ground cinnamon

Cooking Instructions:
1. Preheat air fryer to 330° F.
2. In a small mixing bowl, mix together the cream cheese, sugar, egg, flour and vanilla extract. Put the mixture into the bottom of the tartlet shells.
3. Cook at 330°F for 4 minutes (3 tartlets at a time). Prepare the streusel topping by combining the flour, sugar, cinnamon, walnuts and melted butter in another bowl.
4. Stir the mixture with a fork until it forms small crumbles and set aside. Put 2 tbsp. of the cherry pie filling into each tartlet, on top of the cheese layer.
5. Sprinkle each one with the streusel topping. Add the tartlets back to the Air Fryer in batches and cook at 330° F for 15 minutes.
6. Serve and enjoy!!!

Brownie and Blondie Layer Bars

Preparation Time: 8 minutes
Cooking Time: 18 minutes
Total Time: 26 minutes
Servings: 18- 20 bars

Ingredients:
- ¼ Cup of cocoa powder
- ¼ Cup of flour
- 1 Egg
- ¼ Cup of vegetable oil
- ⅛ Tsp. baking powder
- ⅛ Tsp. salt
- ½ Cup of sugar
- 16 Oz. of your favorite chocolate chip cookie dough

Cooking Instructions:
1. Pre-heat the Air Fryer to 350°F.
2. Place an aluminum foil in your baking pan and spray with melted butter or oil. In an equal layer, place the cookie dough into the bottom of the baking pan.
3. Add the baking pan into the Air Fryer basket. Take a long piece of aluminum foil, folding it in half lengthwise twice until it looks like it is approximately 26-inches by 3-inches.
4. Put this under the baking pan and hold the ends of the foil to enable you move the baking pan in and out of the Air Fryer basket. Cook the dough at 350°F for 8 minutes. Do not cover it while cooking.
5. Mix the brownie batter while the bottom layer is cooking. In a small mixing bowl, mix together the eggs, oil and sugar. In another mixing bowl, mix together the cocoa powder, flour, baking powder and salt.
6. Pour the dry ingredients into the wet ingredients and stir. Put the brownie batter into the cookie layer in the baking pan. Cook the bars at 350° F for 15 minutes.
7. Remove the pan to a cooling rack and allow it to cool in pan for about 8-10 minutes. Cut into 18-20 small squares.
8. Serve and enjoy!!!

Stuffed Apple Pies

Preparation Time: 8 minutes
Cooking Time: 12 minutes
Total Time: 20 minutes
Servings: 4

Ingredients:
- ¼ Tsp. ground ginger
- 1 Tsp. ground cinnamon
- 2 Gala apples, peeled and finely diced
- 3 Tbsp. sugar
- 1 Egg, beaten
- Coarse sanding sugar
- Pinch of nutmeg
- 2 Tbsp. butter, cut into 4 slices
- 4 Large Granny Smith apples
- Juice of 1 lemon
- 2 Ready-made pie dough

Cooking Instructions:
1. Using a paring knife, remove the top of the Granny Smith apples and cut around the inside edge of the apple, leaving a ¼-inch border of apple next to the skin.
2. Remove the inside of the apple with a spoon, discard the core and seeds, and squeeze lemon juice on the inside of the apples and set aside.
3. Pre-heat a skillet on medium heat. Add the butter and sauté the apple pulp along with the diced apples, sugar, nutmeg, cinnamon and ginger for 2 to 3 minutes.
4. Fill the apple shells with the sautéed apple mixture. Divide the pie dough into 16 strips (1¼ -inch x 4½-inch). Place 2 strips across the top of each apple.
5. Keep the other 2 strips in the opposite direction over the apple and then brush the dough strips with a little beaten egg and spray the sanding sugar on top.
6. Pre-heat the Air Fryer to 350°F. Put the apples in the Air Fryer basket and cook at 350°F for 12 minutes. Top with whipped cream.
7. Serve and enjoy!!!

Peach and Blueberry Cobbler

Preparation Time: 10 minutes
Cooking Time: 80 minutes
Total Time: 1 hour 30 minutes
Servings: 4

Ingredients:
- Juice of half a lemon
- ⅓ Cup of sugar
- 3 Cups of sliced, peeled peaches (fresh or frozen and thawed)
- 3 Tbsp. cornstarch
- Pinch of salt
- 2 Cups of blueberries (fresh or frozen and thawed)

Topping:
- ¾ Cup of all-purpose flour
- 3 Tbsp. butter, cold
- ⅔ Cup of Buttermilk
- 1 Tsp. baking powder
- 4 Tbsp. sugar
- Turbinado sugar
- ¼ Tsp. salt

Instructions:
1. In a large mixing bowl, mix together the sugar, cornstarch and a pinch of salt.
2. Add the peaches, blueberries and lemon juice and mix the fruit thoroughly to coat everything with the sugar mixture. Turn the fruit into a 7-inch baking pan.
3. In a large mixing bowl, stir together the flour, baking powder, salt and sugar. Grate the butter into the flour and stir it in to coat evenly. Stir in the buttermilk.
4. Pre-heat the Air Fryer to 380°F. Put the batter over the top of the fruit. Spray the Turbinado sugar over the batter.
5. Wrap the cake pan with aluminum foil, leaving a dome on the top so that the foil doesn't touch the dollops of batter and put it into the Air Fryer basket.
6. Cook at 380°F for 65 minutes. Get the aluminum foil out and cook at 330°F for another 15 minutes.
7. Serve and enjoy!!!

Chocolate Soufflés

Preparation Time: 10 minutes
Cooking Time: 14 minutes
Total Time: 24 minutes
Servings: 2

Ingredients:
- 2 Eggs, separated
- 3 Tbsp. sugar
- 3 Oz. semi-sweet chocolate, chopped
- ½ Tsp. pure vanilla extract
- 2 Tbsp. all-purpose flour
- Powdered sugar, for dusting the finished soufflés
- ¼ Cup of butter
- Heavy cream (for serving)

Cooking Instructions:
1. Spray butter and sugar on two 6 Oz. ramekins.
2. In a microwave, melt the chocolate and butter together. Beat the egg yolks in a separate bowl.
3. Put the sugar and the vanilla extract and beat well again. Sprinkle the chocolate and butter, Stir in the flour. Mix properly.
4. Pre-heat the air fryer to 330°F. In a mixing bowl, whisk the egg whites and fold the whipped egg whites into the chocolate mixture in batches.
5. Gently turn the batter to the buttered ramekins, leaving about ½-inch at the top. Put the ramekins into the Air Fryer basket and cook for 14 minutes.
6. Dust with powdered sugar. Serve immediately and enjoy!!!

Fried Banana S'mores

Preparation Time: 5 minutes
Cooking Time: 6 minutes
Total Time: 11 minutes
Servings: 2

Ingredients:
- 3 Tbsp. mini peanut butter chips
- 3 Tbsp. mini marshmallows
- 4 Bananas
- 3 Tbsp. mini semi-sweet chocolate chips
- 3 Tbsp. graham cracker cereal

Instructions:
1. Pre-heat the Air Fryer to 400°F.
2. Cut the un-peeled bananas lengthwise along the inside of the curve, you do not need to cut through the bottom of the peel.
3. Slightly open the banana to form a pocket. Fill each pocket with marshmallows, peanut butter chips and chocolate chips.
4. Add the graham cracker cereal into the filling. Put the bananas into the Air Fryer basket.
5. Let them rest on each other and make the filling to face up. Cook at 330° F for 6 minutes.
6. Serve and enjoy!!!

Midnight Nutella Banana Sandwich

Preparation Time: 5 minutes
Cooking Time: 8 minutes
Total Time: 13 minutes
Servings: 2

Ingredients:
- 1 Banana
- Butter, softened
- ¼ Cup of chocolate hazelnut spread
- 4 Slices of white bread

Instructions:
1. Pre-heat the Air Fryer to 370°F.
2. Put the softened butter on one side of all the slices of bread and turn the buttered side down.
3. Put the chocolate hazelnut spread on the other side of the bread slices. Divide the banana in half and then slice each half into three slices lengthwise.
4. Put the banana slices on two slices of bread and top with the remaining slices of bread in order to make two sandwiches.
5. Cut the sandwiches in half to help them fit in the Air Fryer at once. Put the sandwiches to the Air Fryer.
6. Cook at 370°F for 5 minutes. Flip them over to the other side and cook for another 3 minutes.
7. Serve and enjoy!!!

www.ingramcontent.com/pod-product-compliance
Lightning Source LLC
Chambersburg PA
CBHW081745100526
44592CB00015B/2304